Dear explorers of nature,

May this book be more than just a pastime, but rather a gateway
to a world of discovery and learning about the importance
of caring for our planet and all beings that inhabit it.

With love and gratitude for the beauty of nature,

Lizz Sampaio

2024

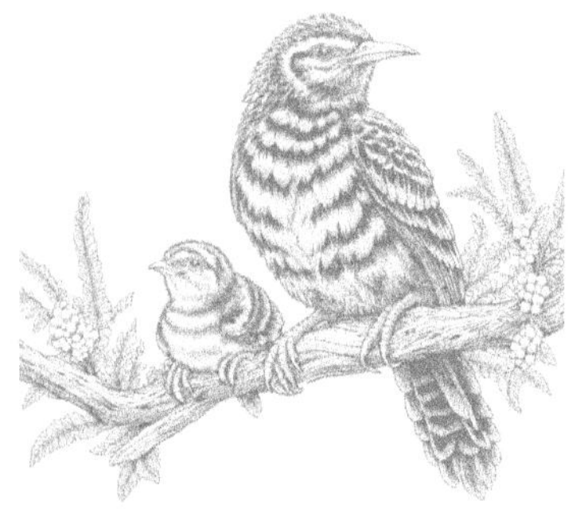

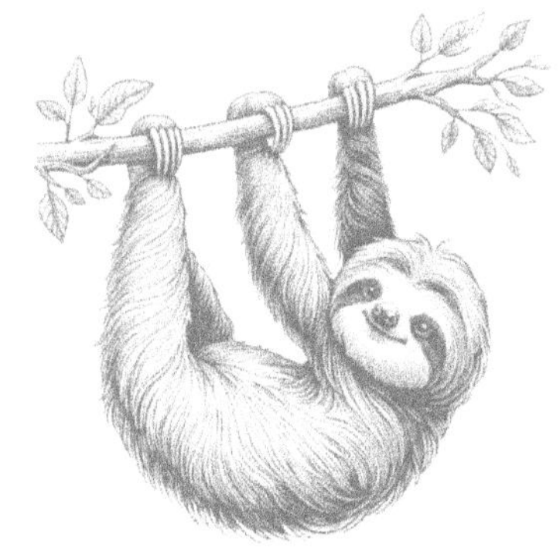

I,_______________________ ,will be coloring
with great joy, this wonderful book of animals from
the Atlantic Forest!

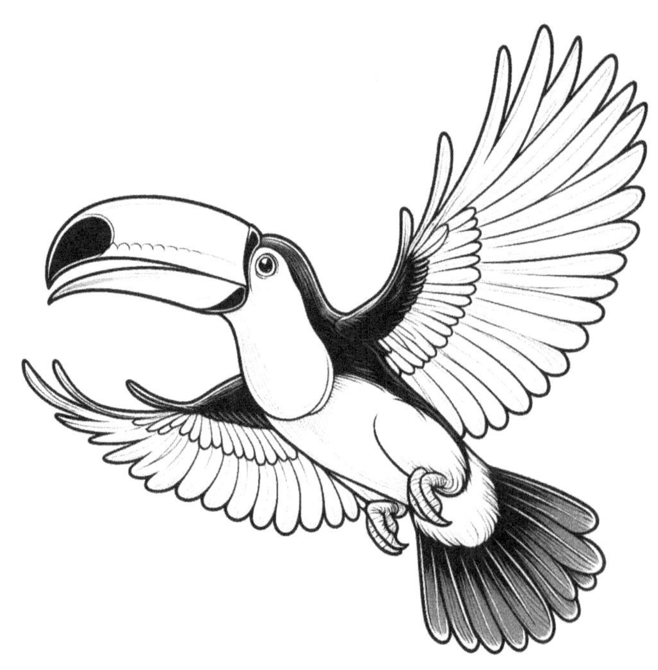

TEST COLOR PAGE

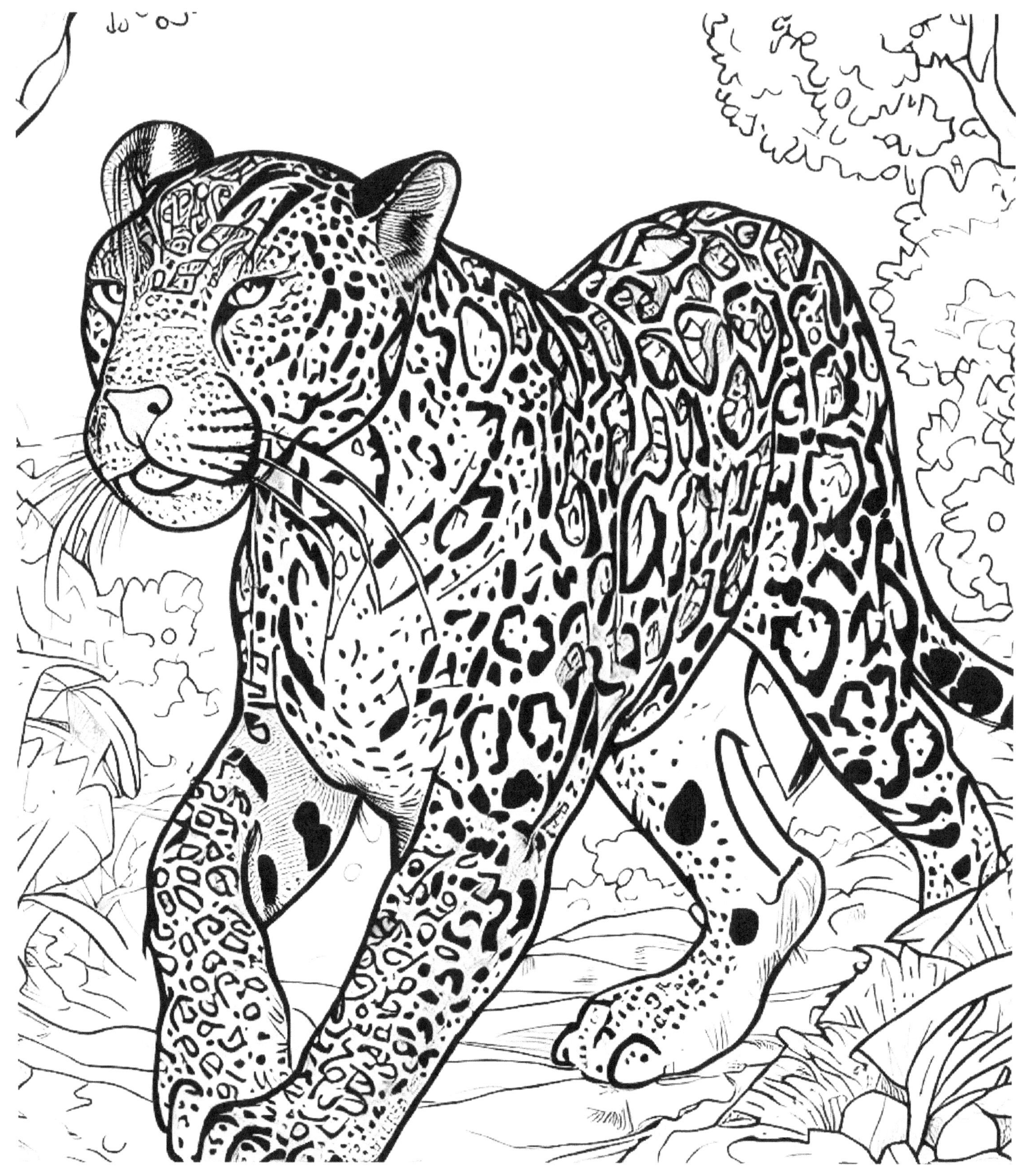
JAGUAR
JAGUAR

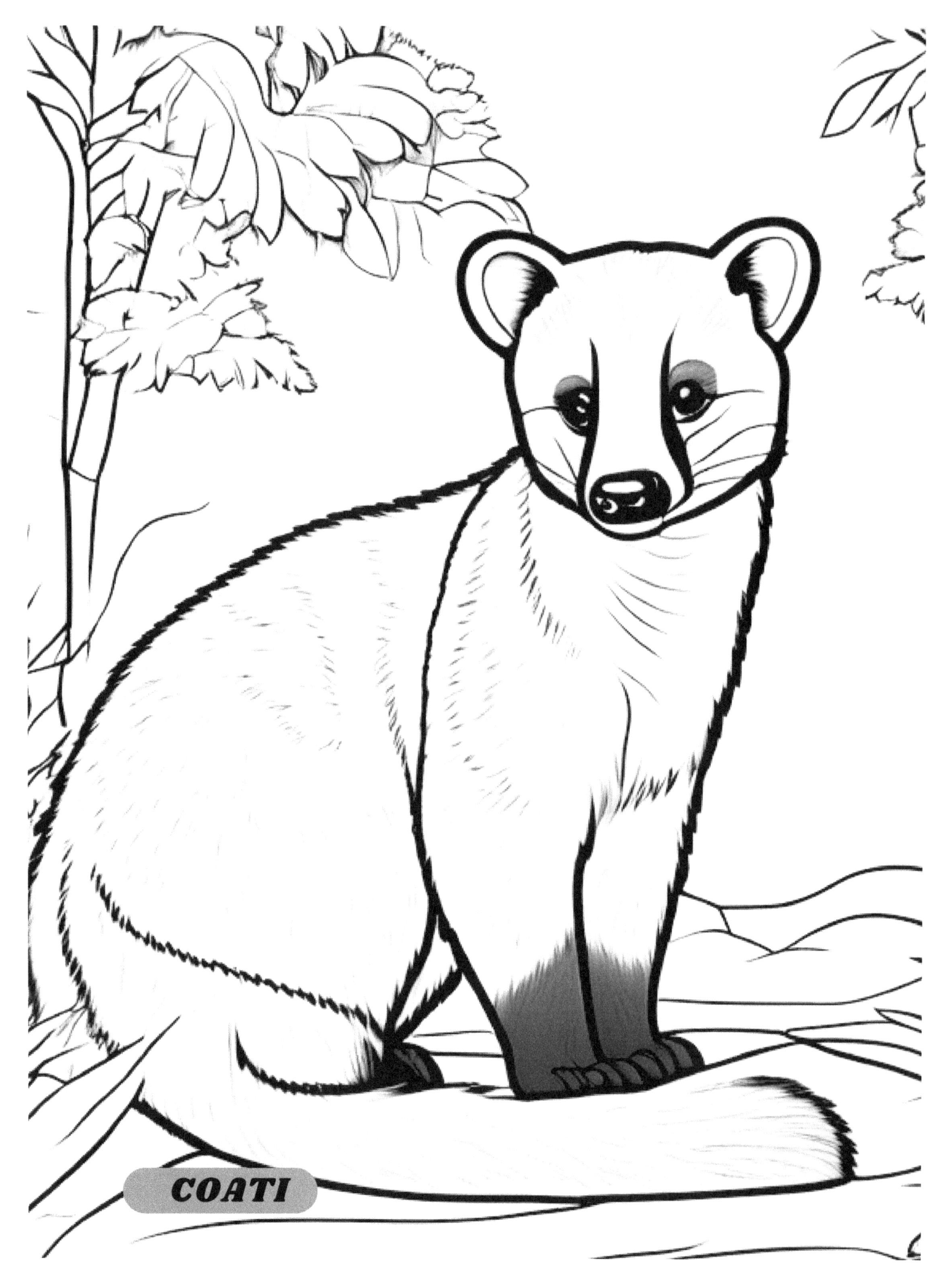
COATI

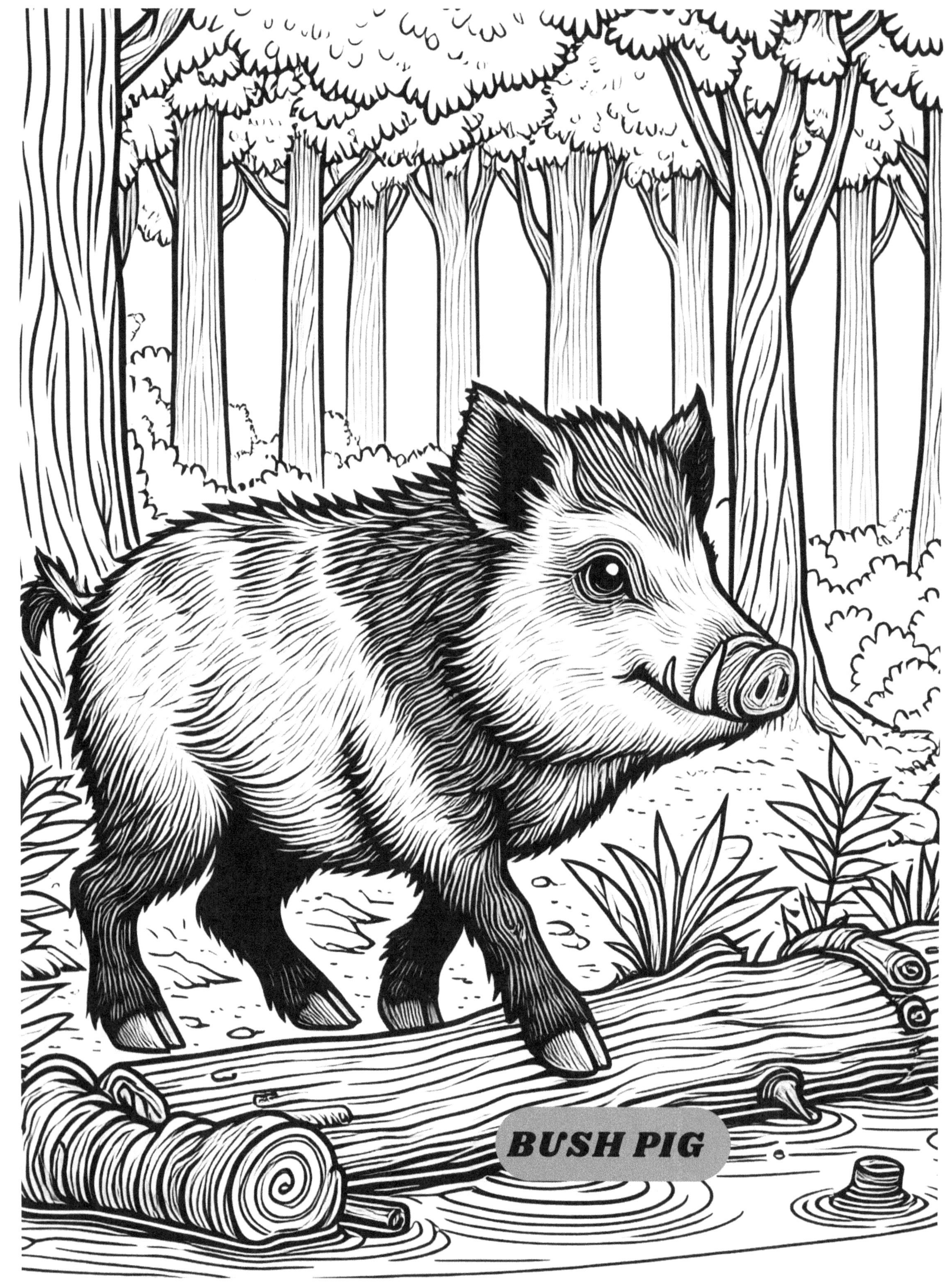
BUSH PIG

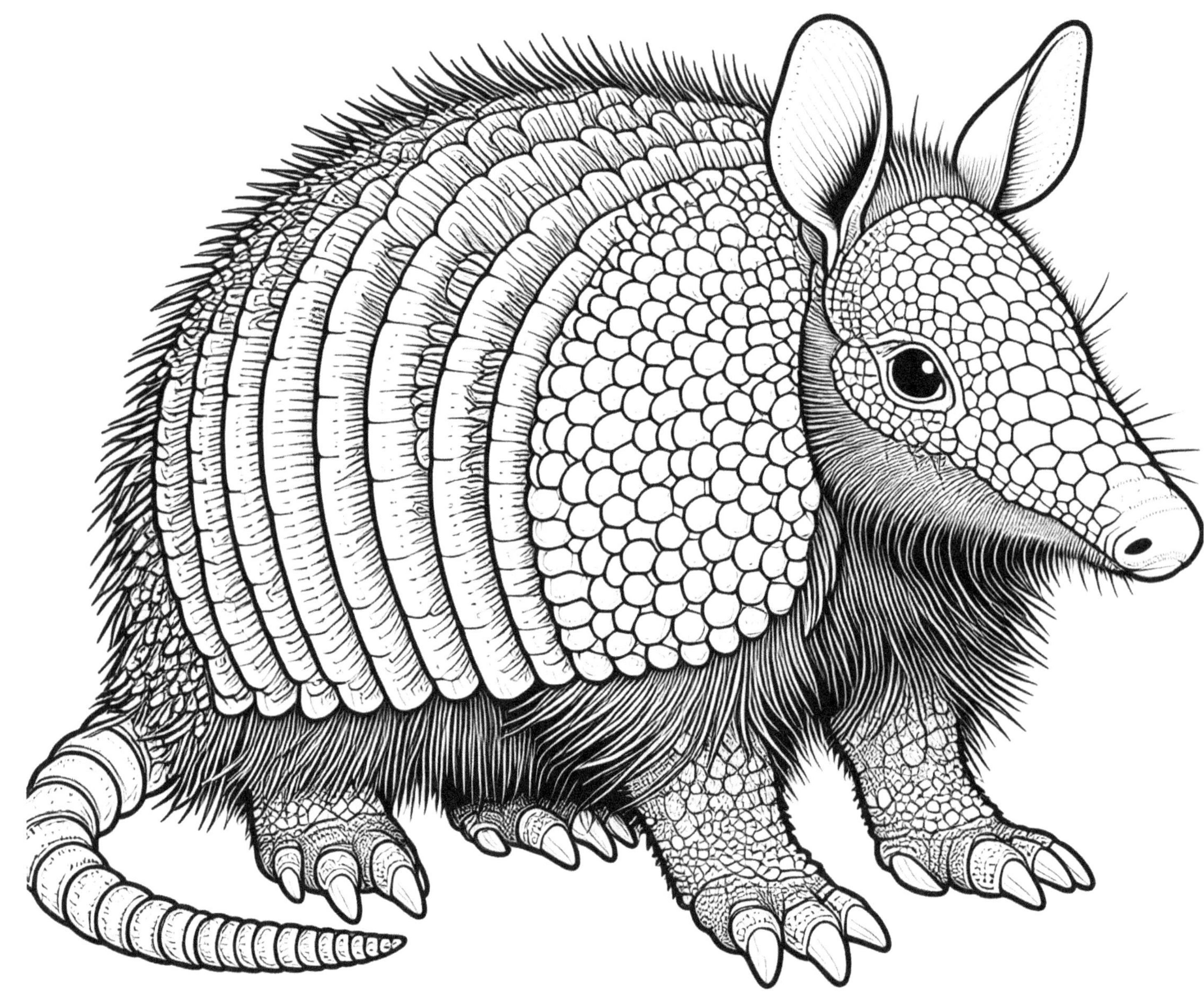

HAIRY TATU

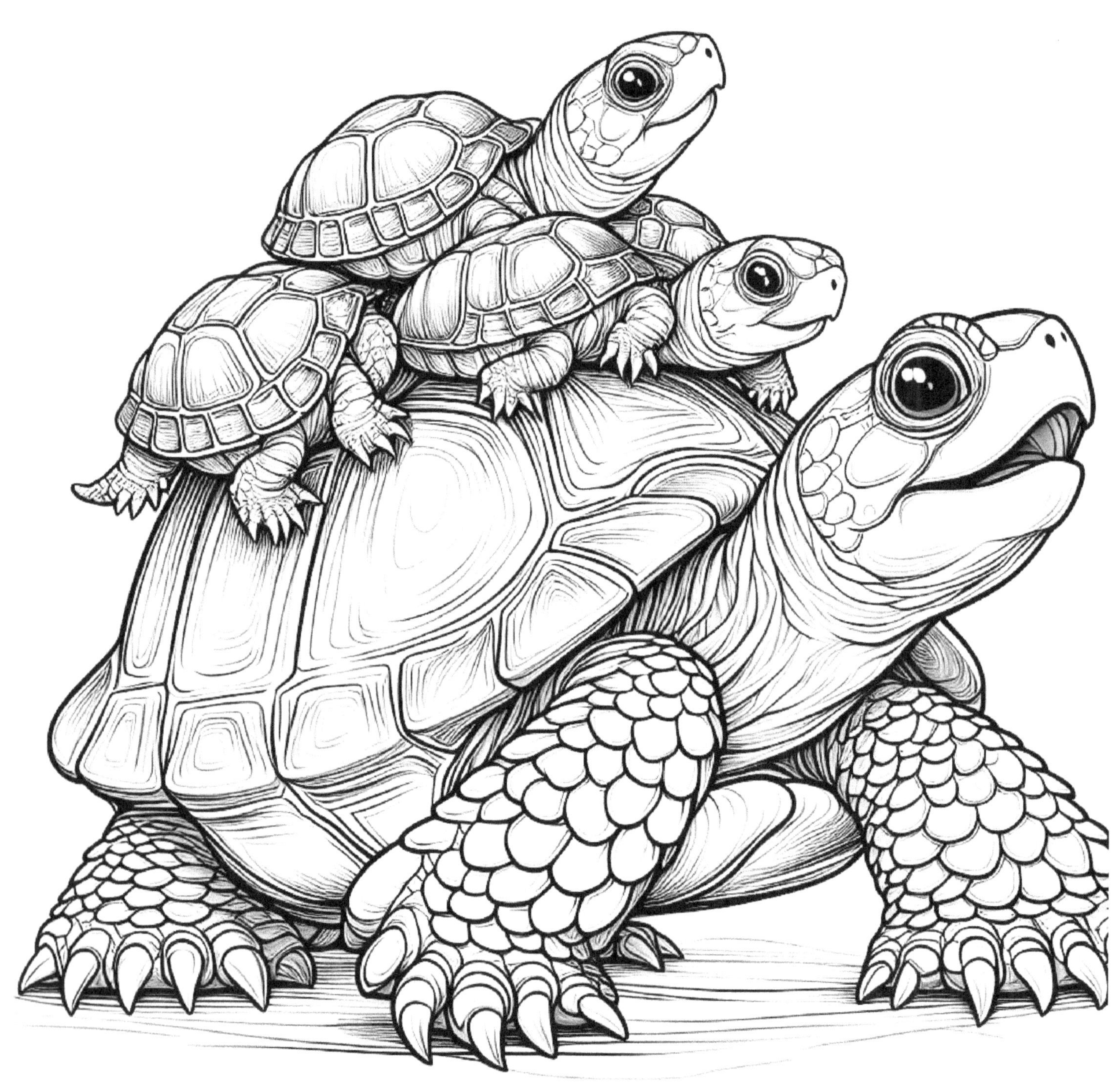

ATLANTIC TURTLE

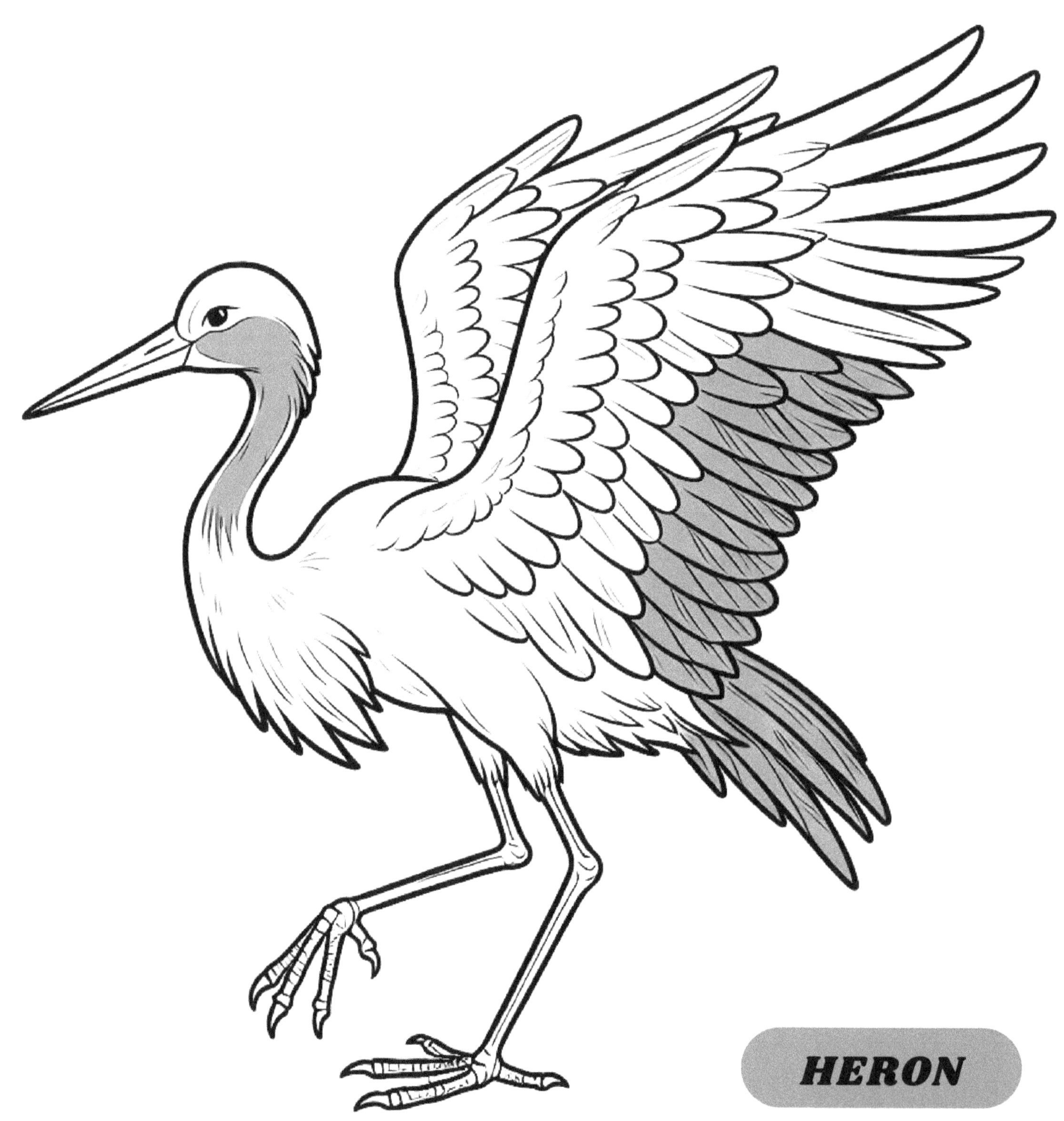

HERON

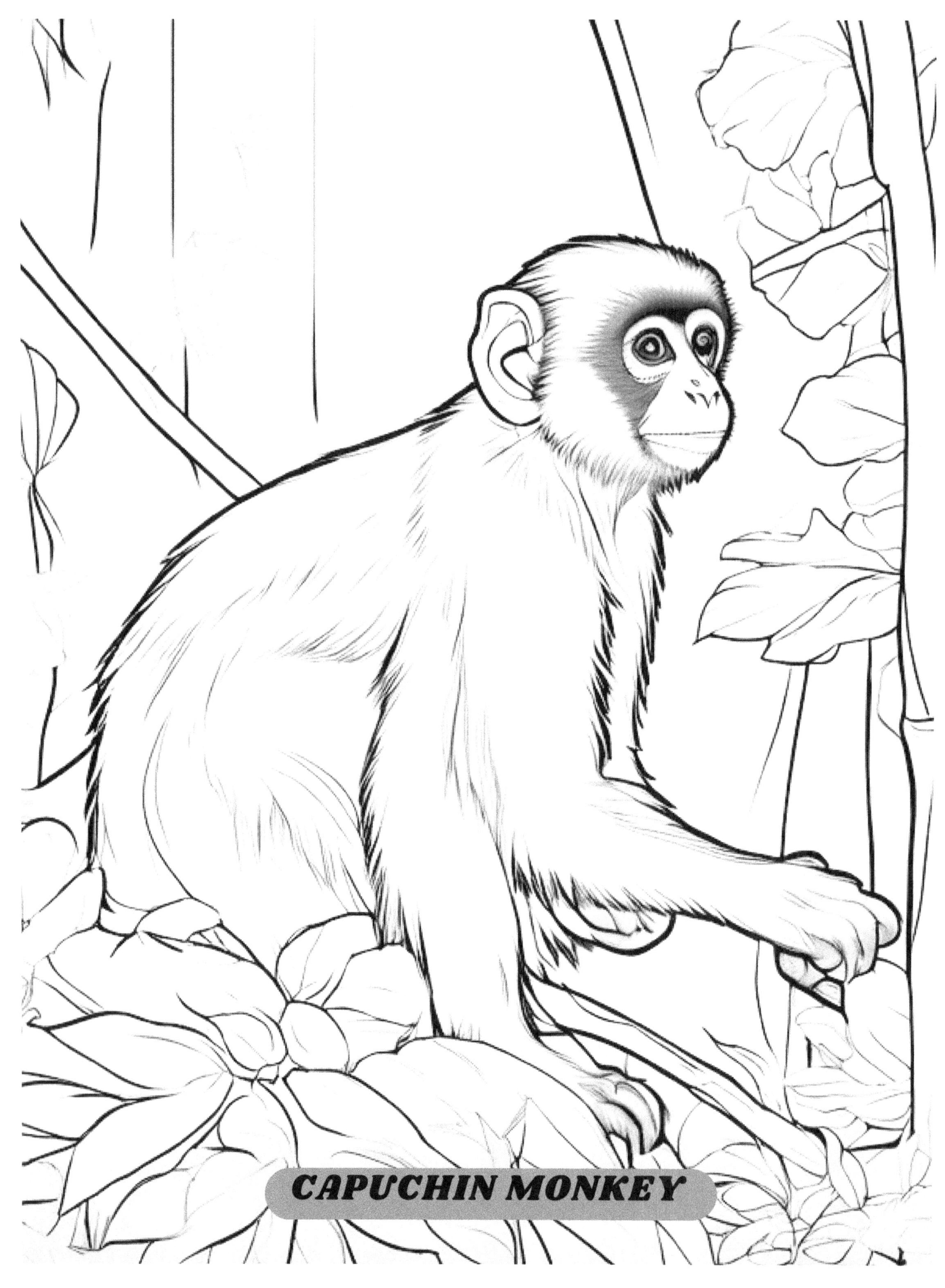

CAPUCHIN MONKEY

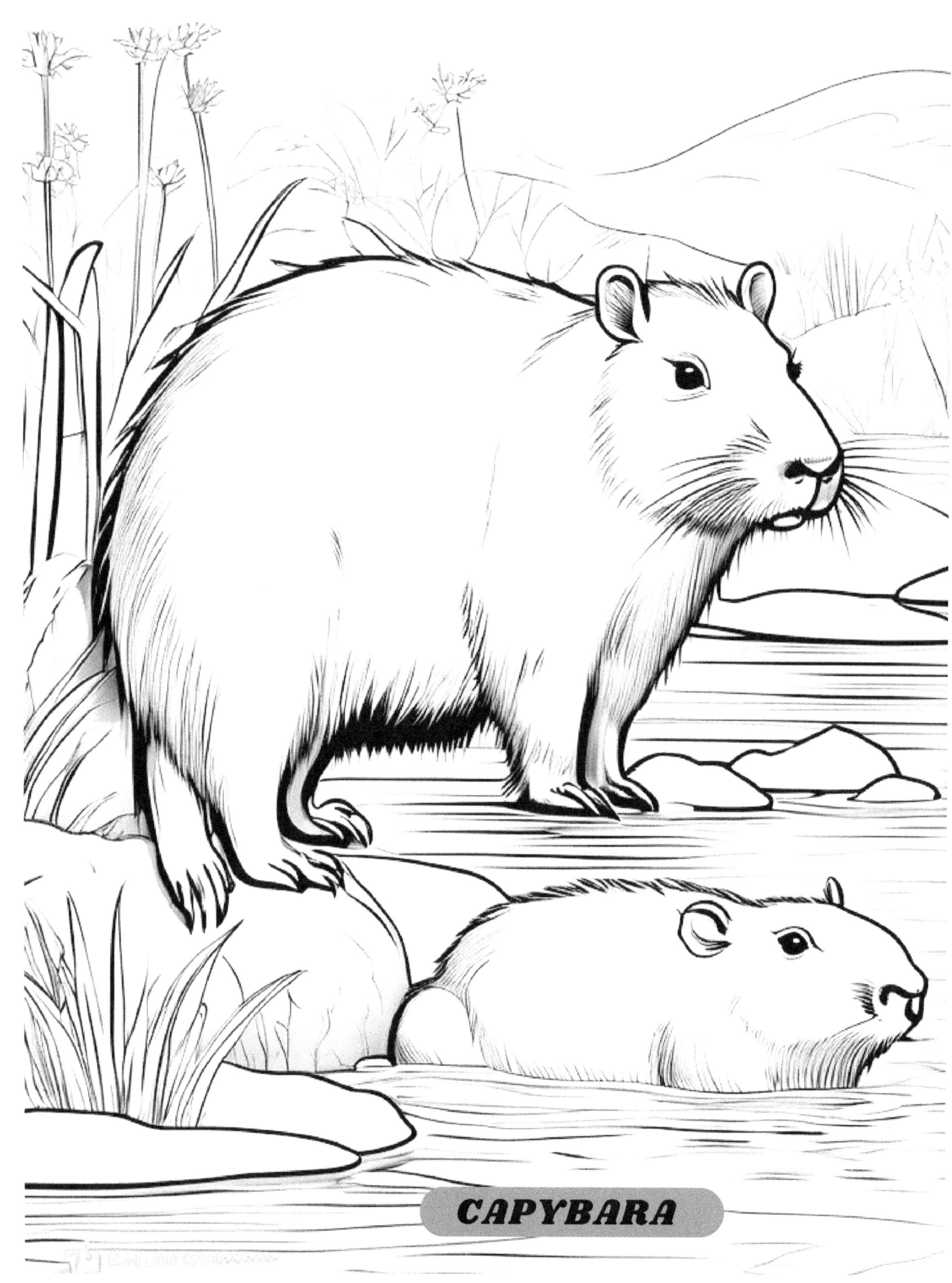

CAPYBARA

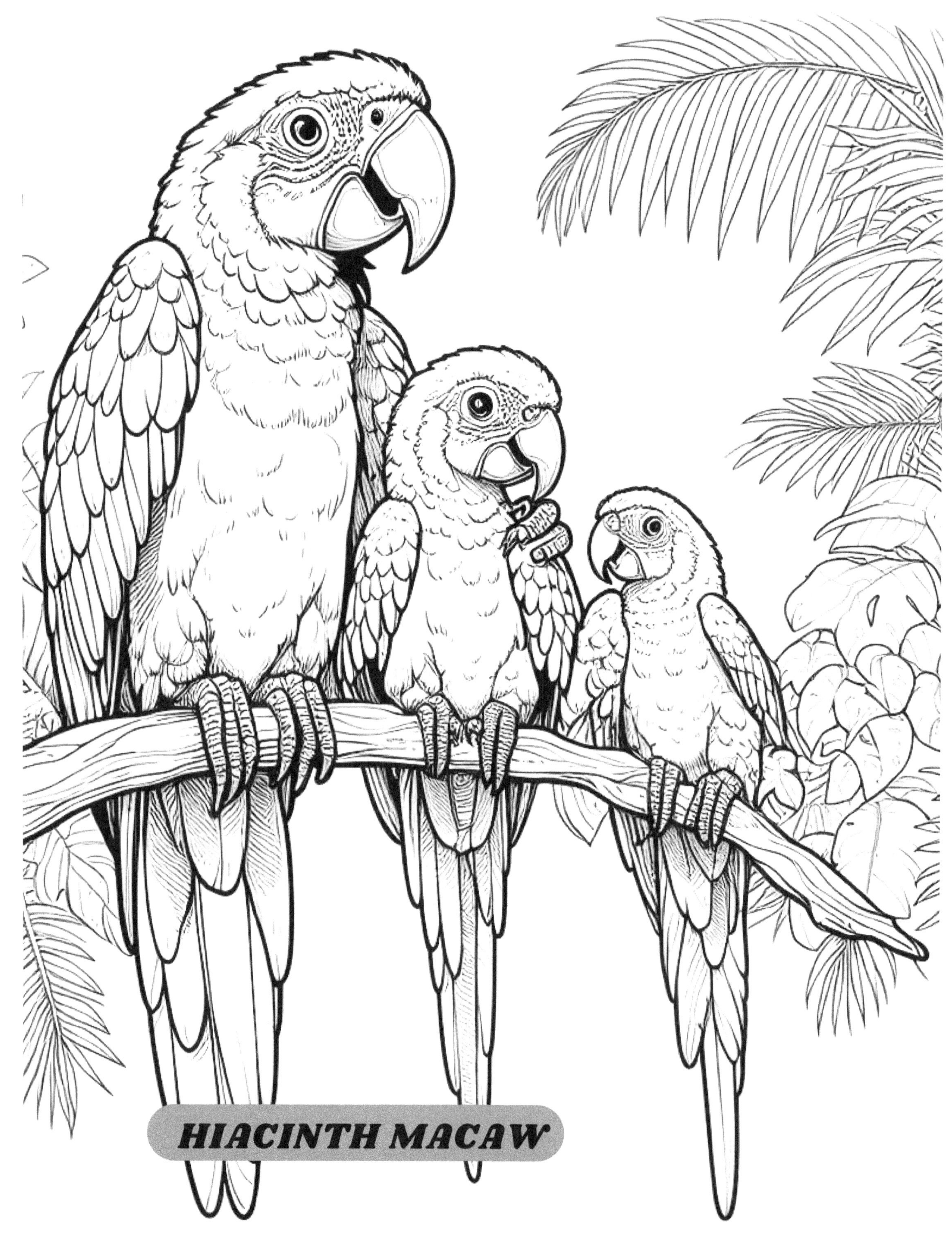
HIACINTH MACAW

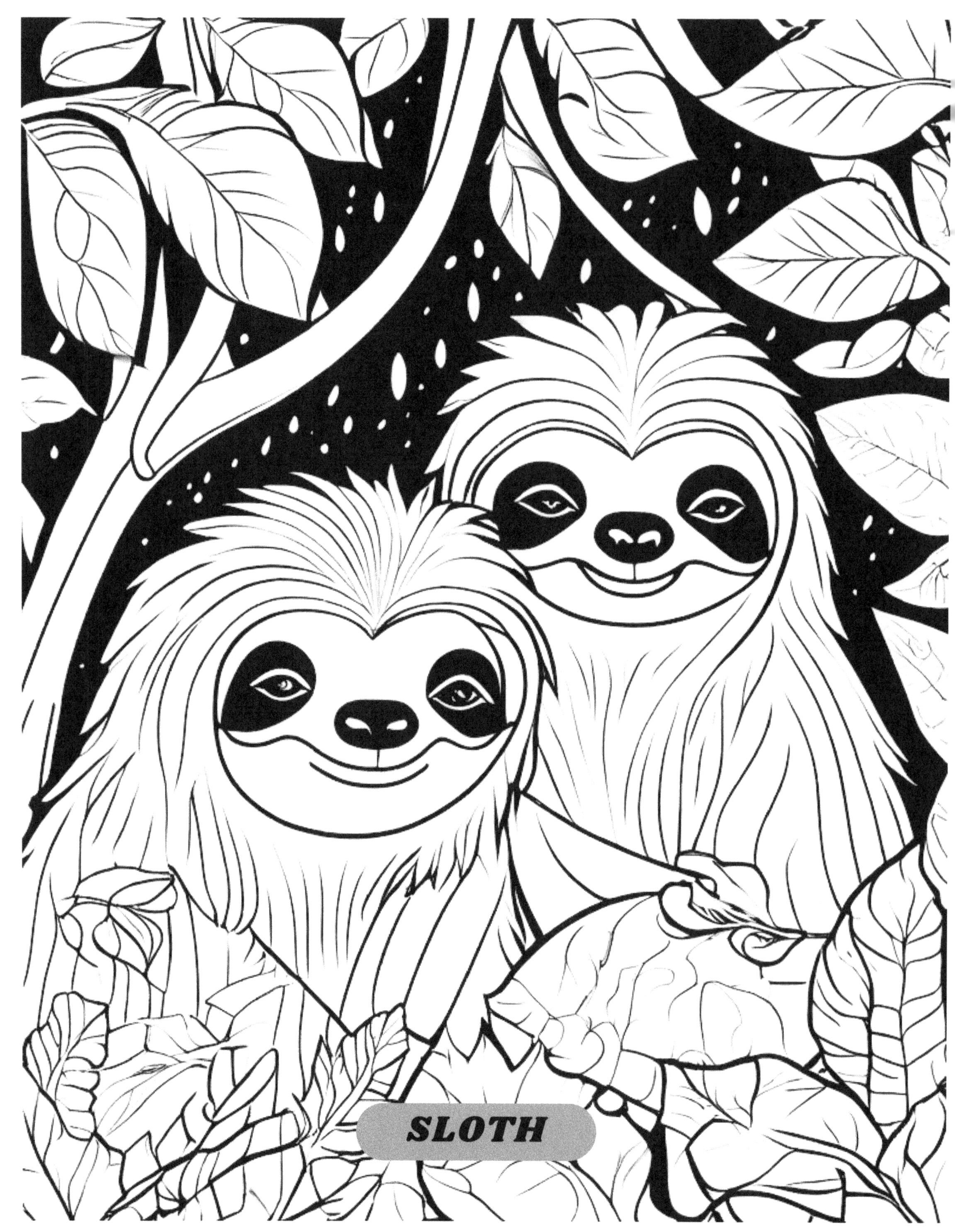

SLOTH

YELLOW-BELLIED ALLIGATOR

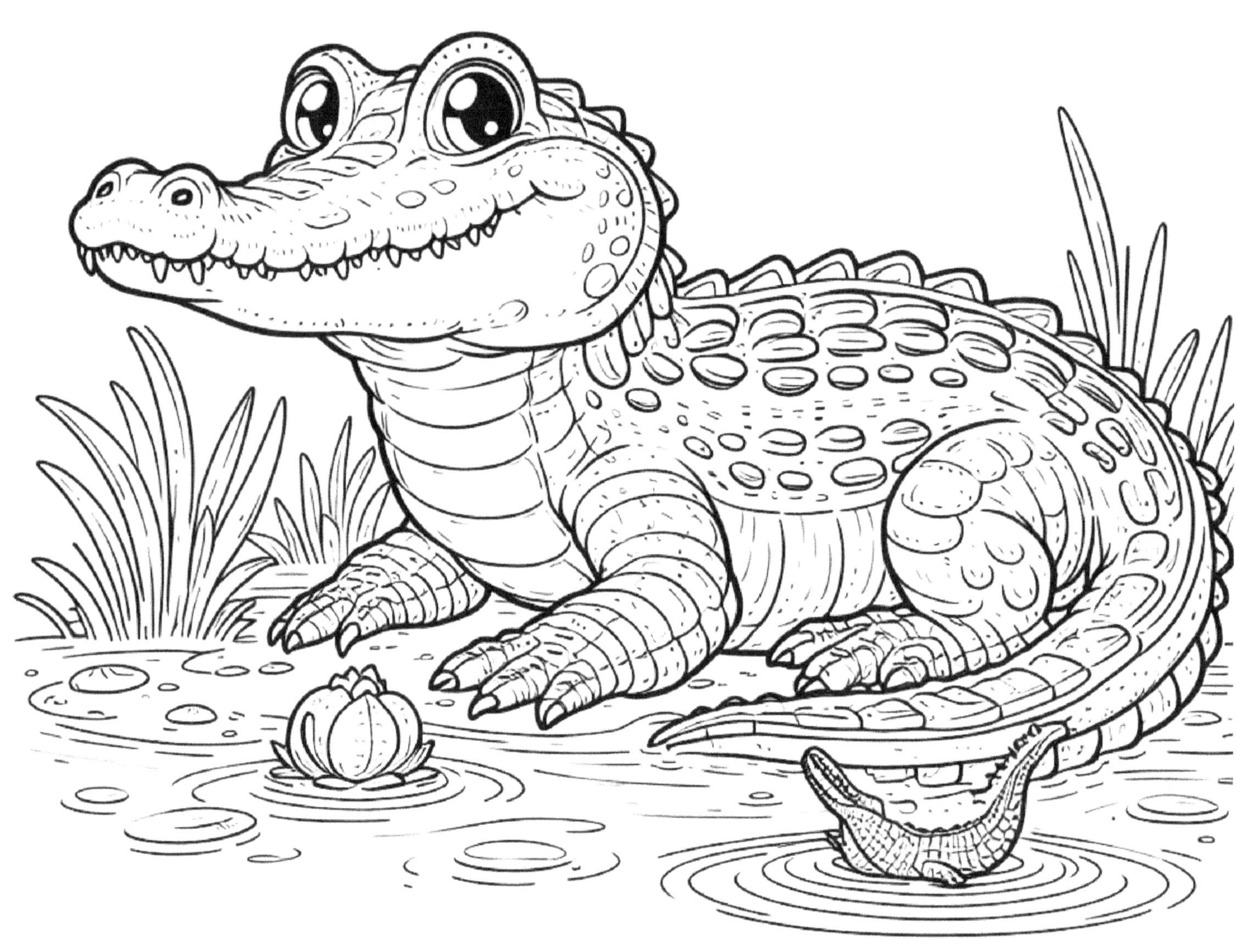

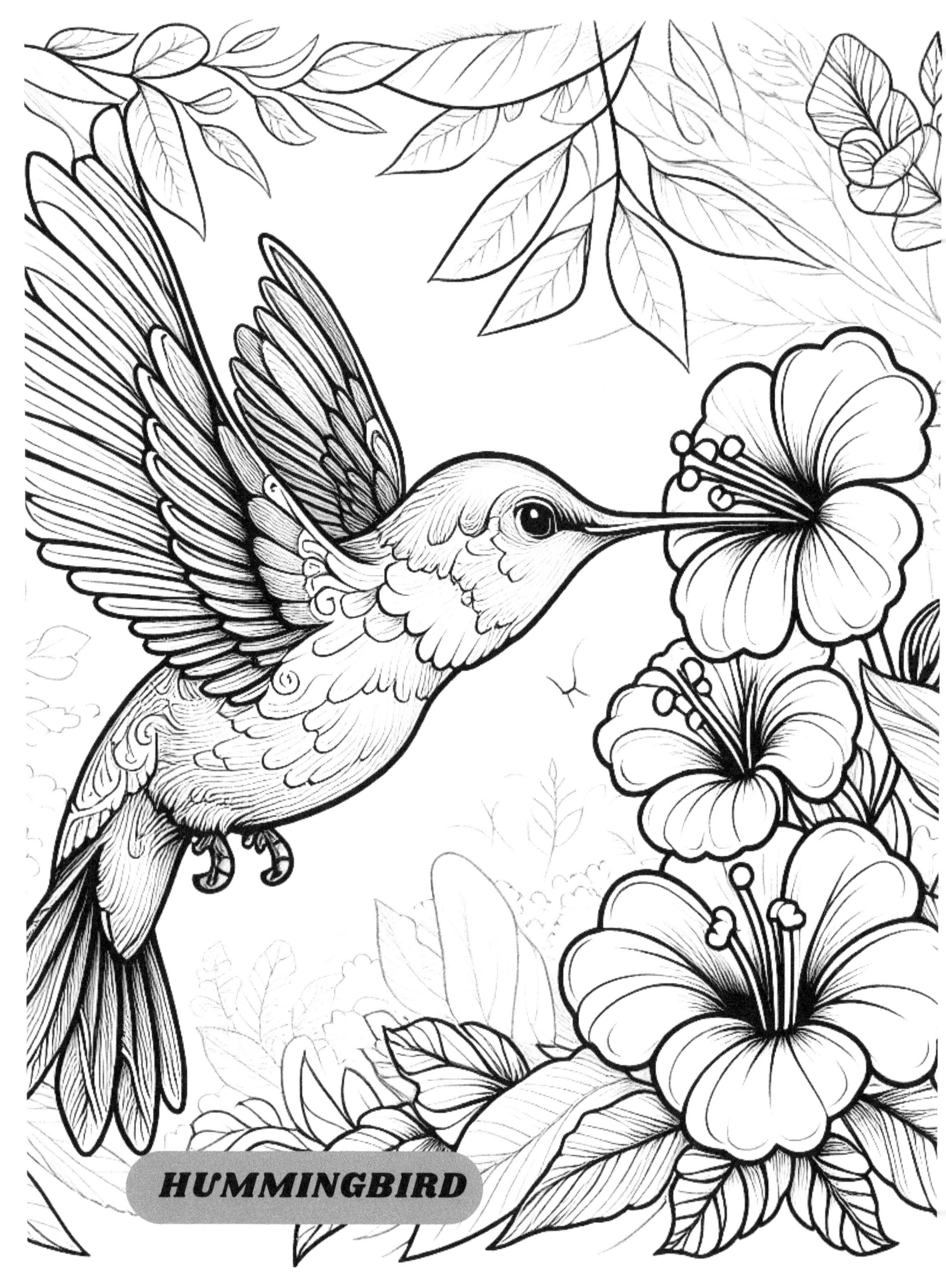

HUMMINGBIRD

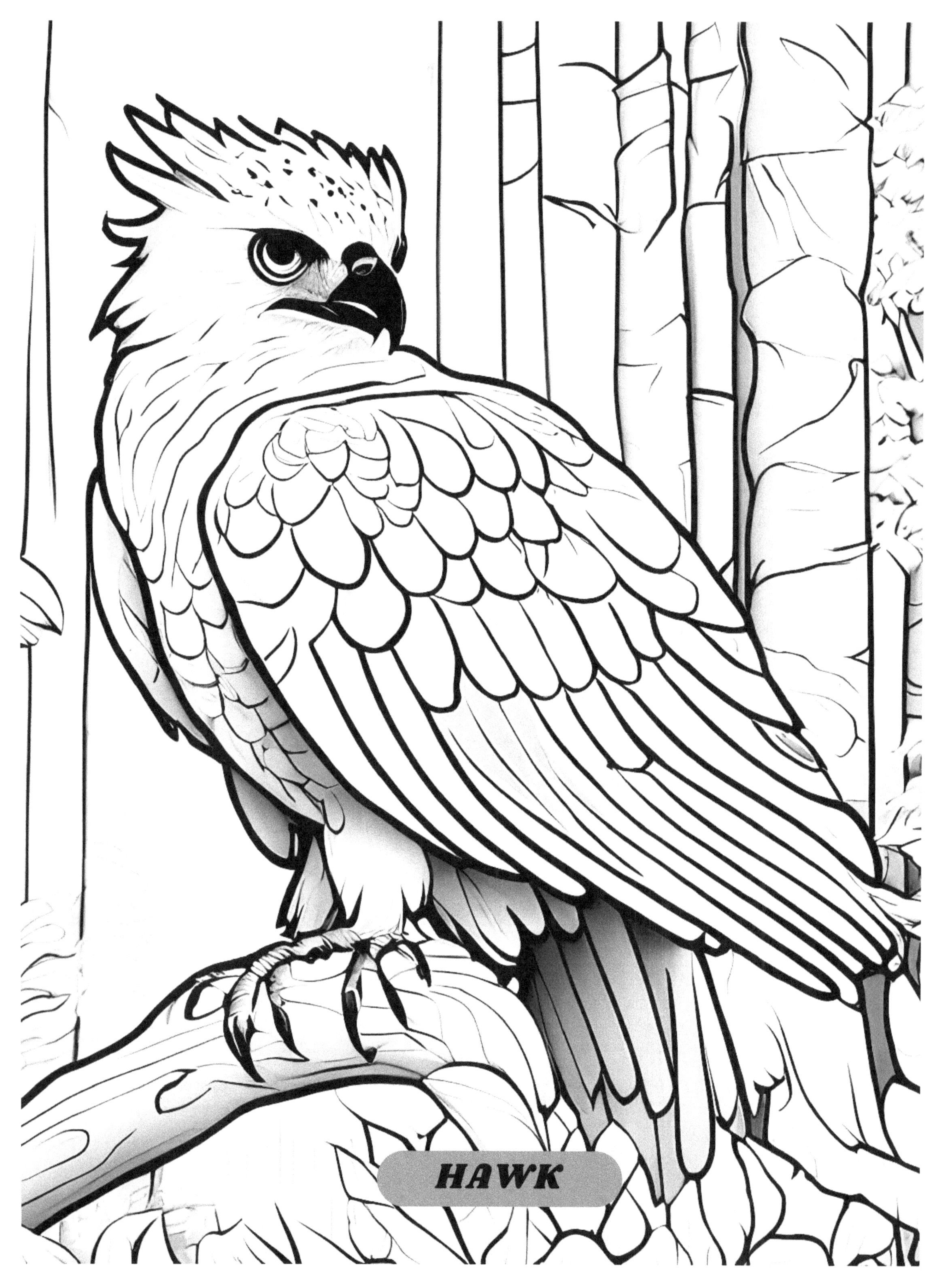
HAWK

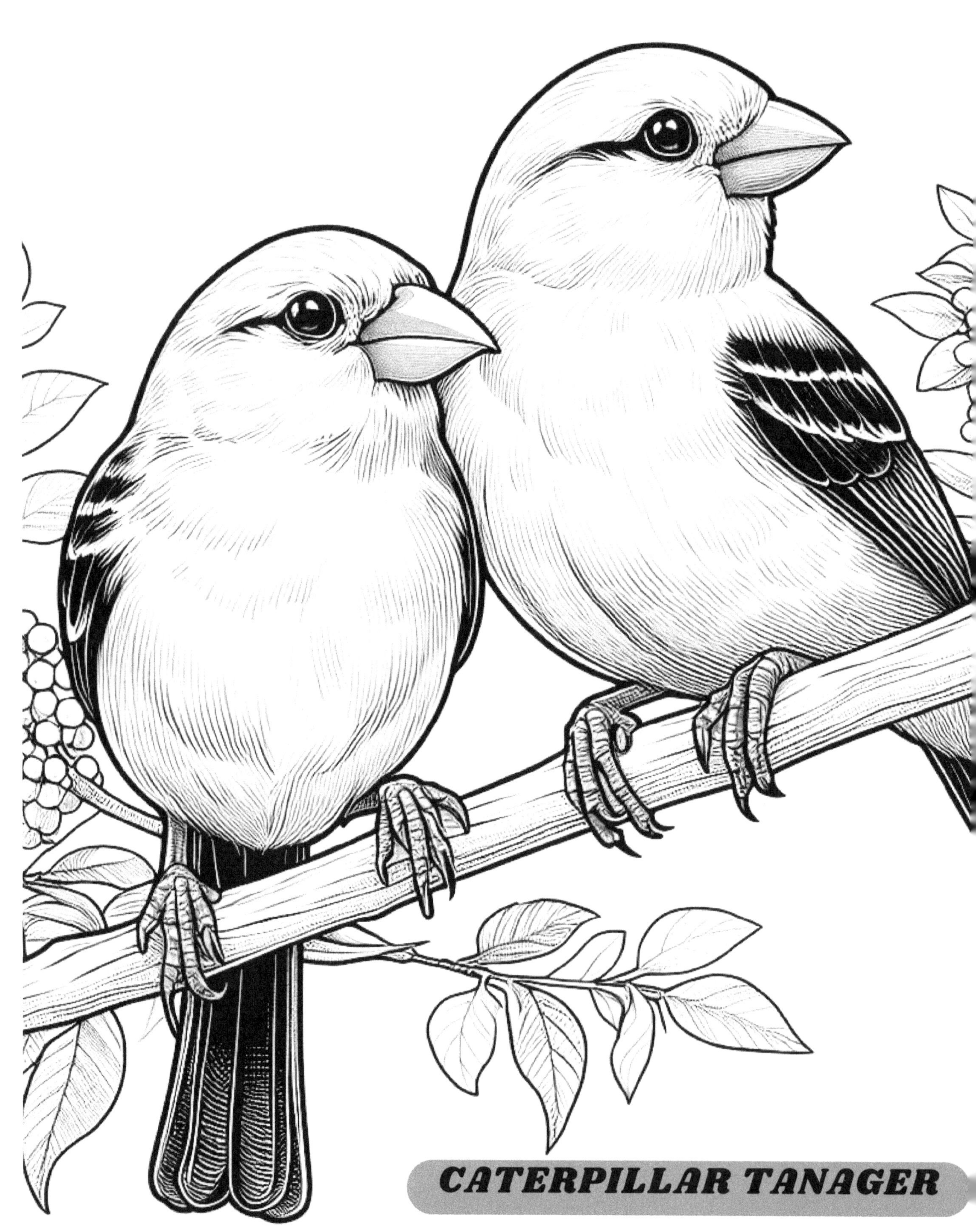

CATERPILLAR TANAGER

JAGUARITIRA

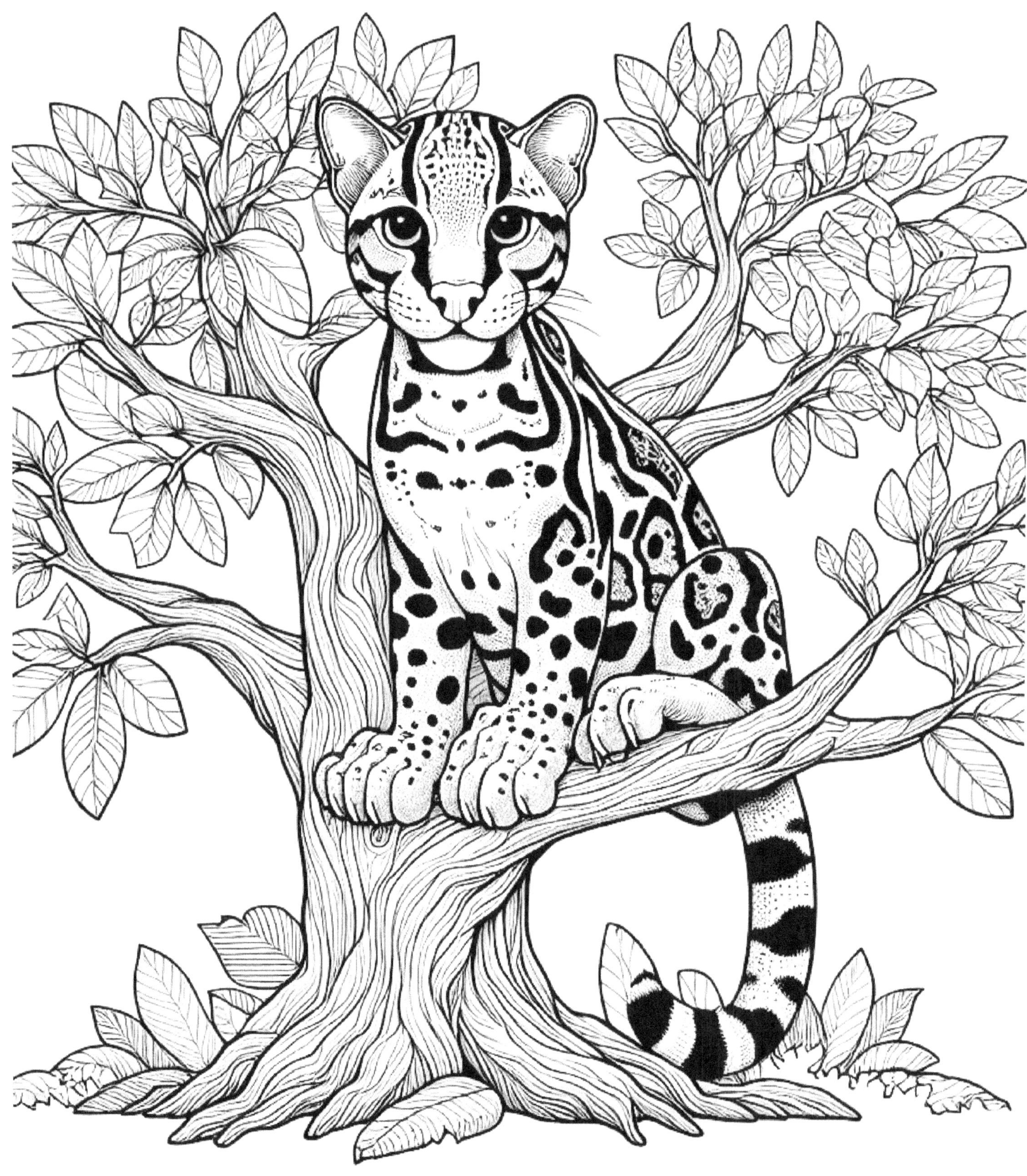

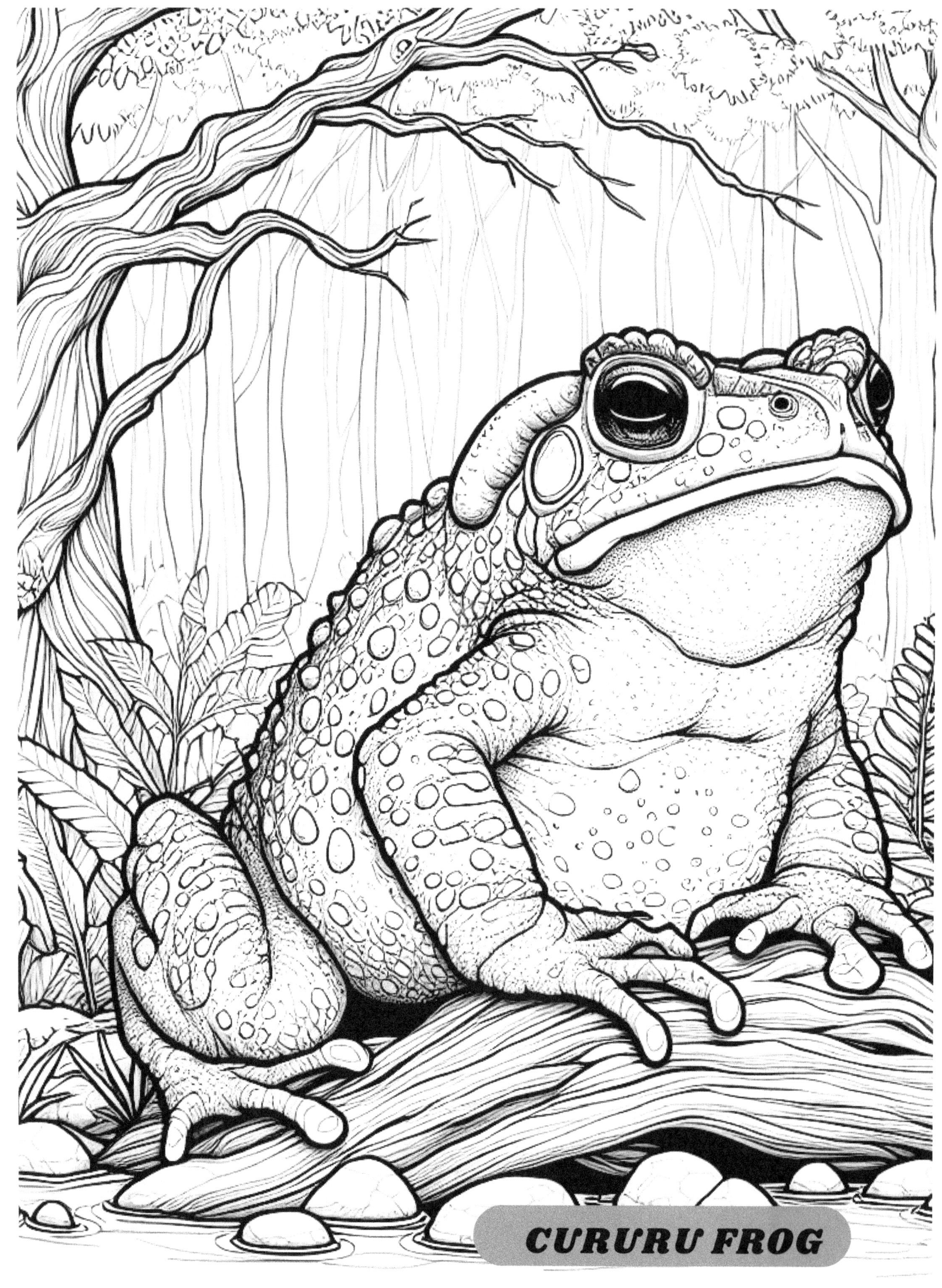
CURURU FROG

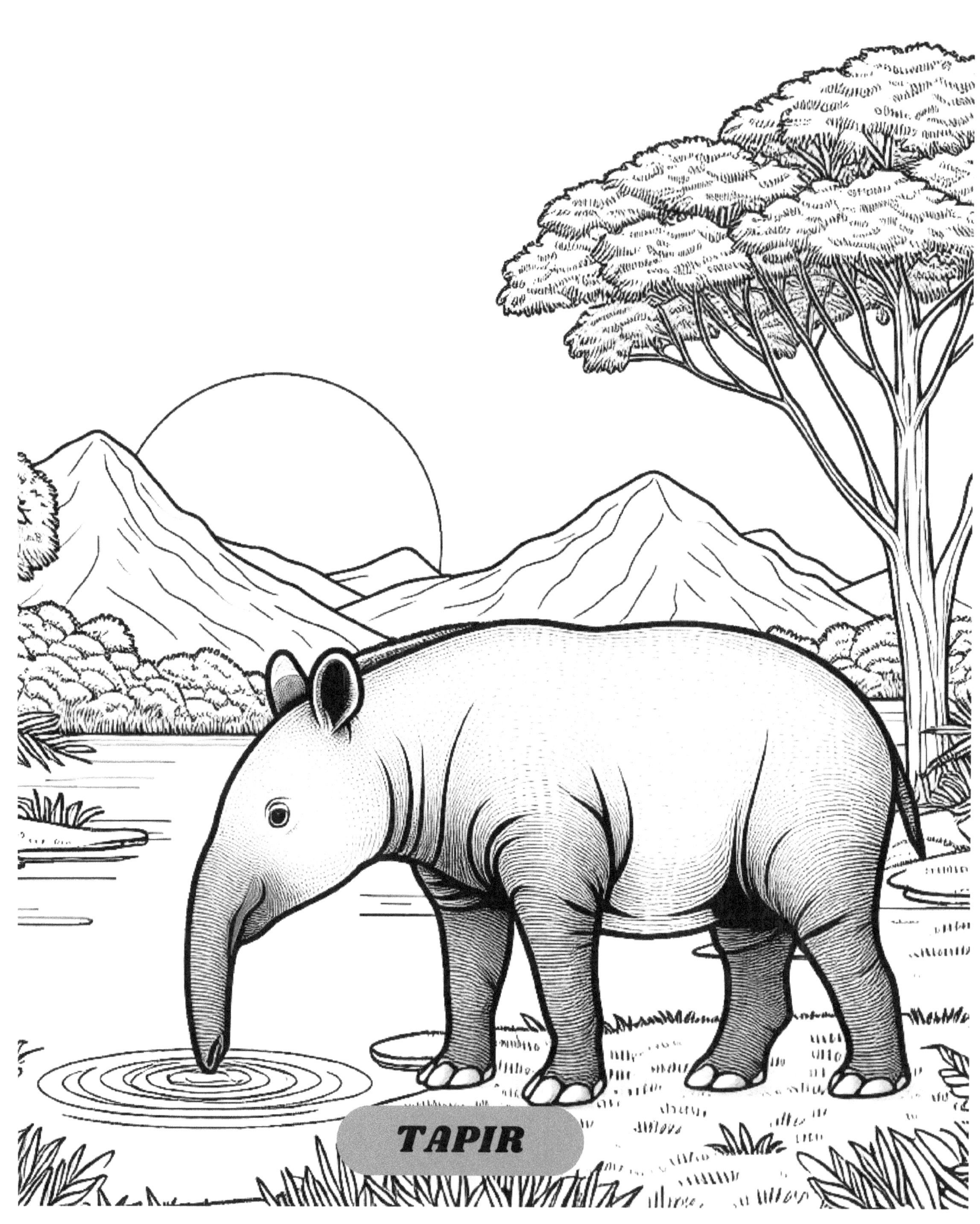
TAPIR

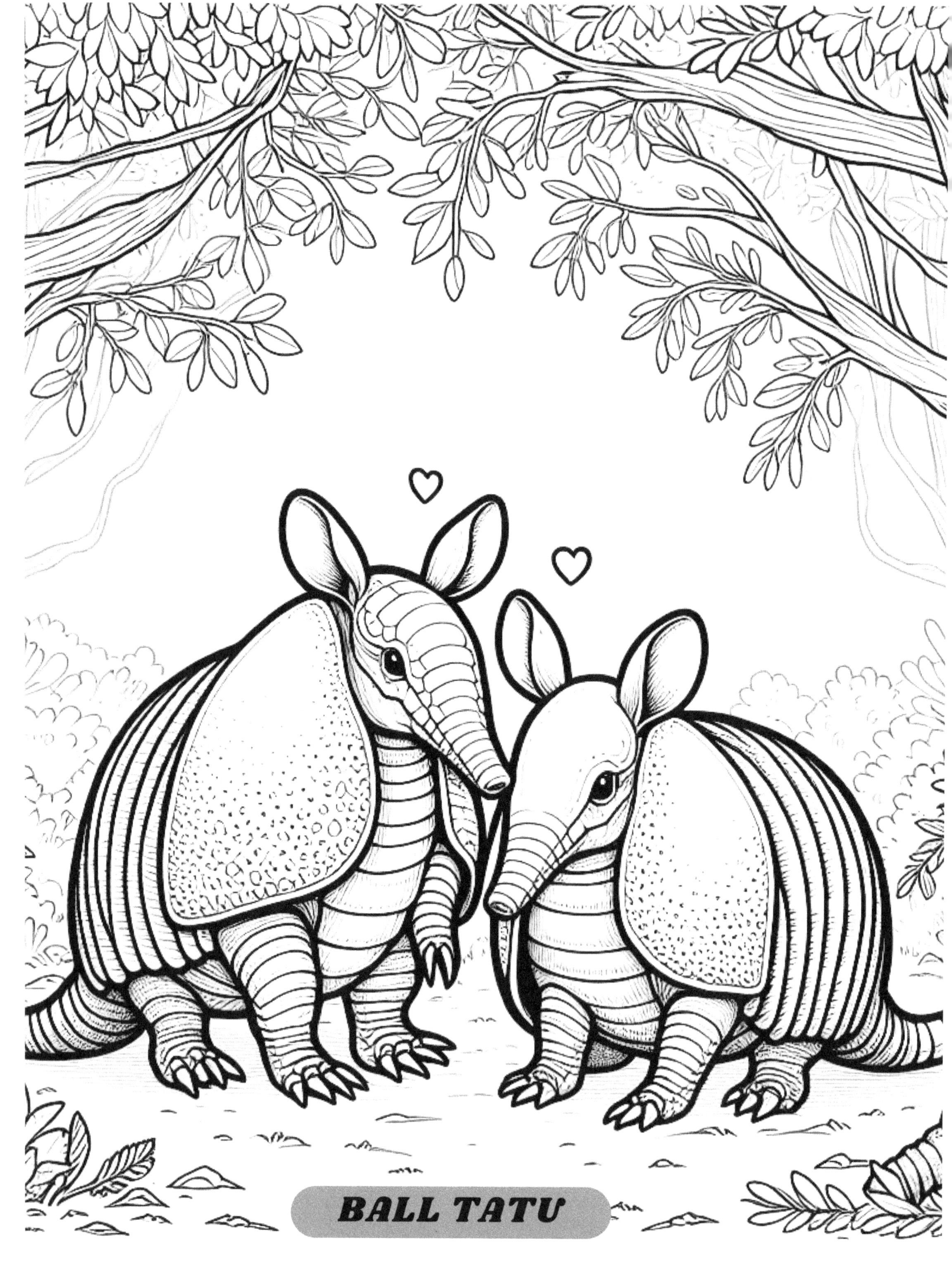
BALL TATU

FLAG ANTEATER

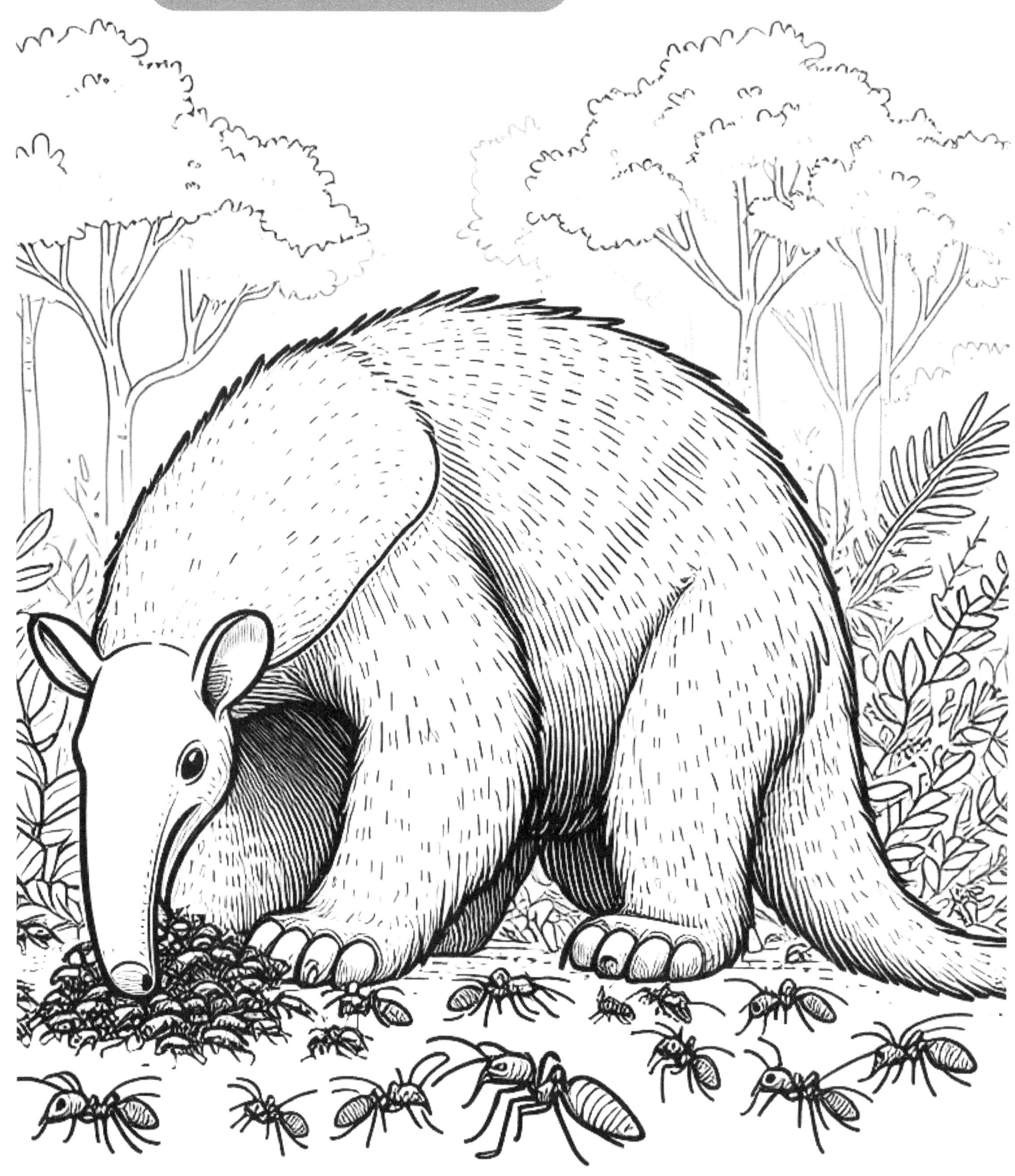

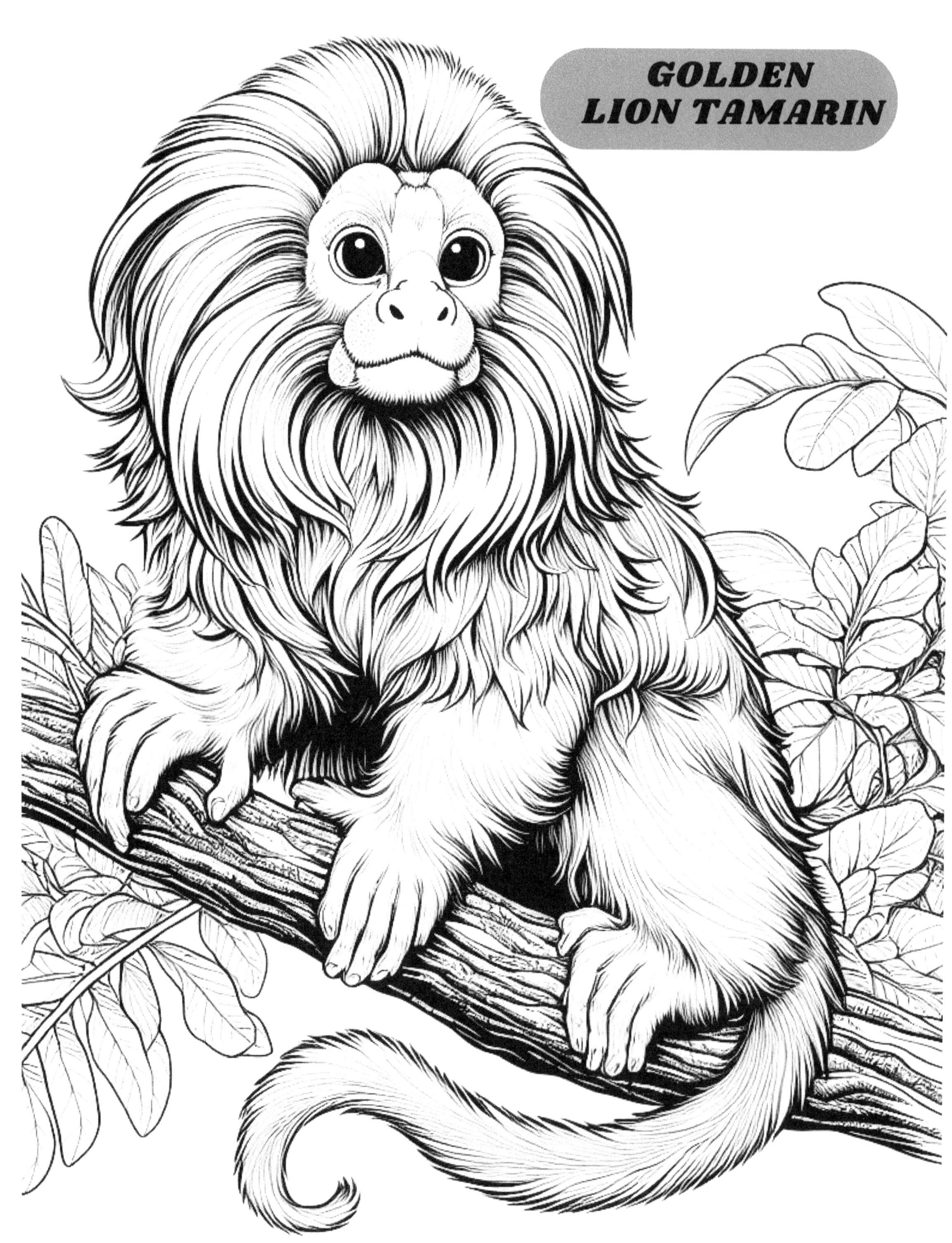
GOLDEN
LION TAMARIN

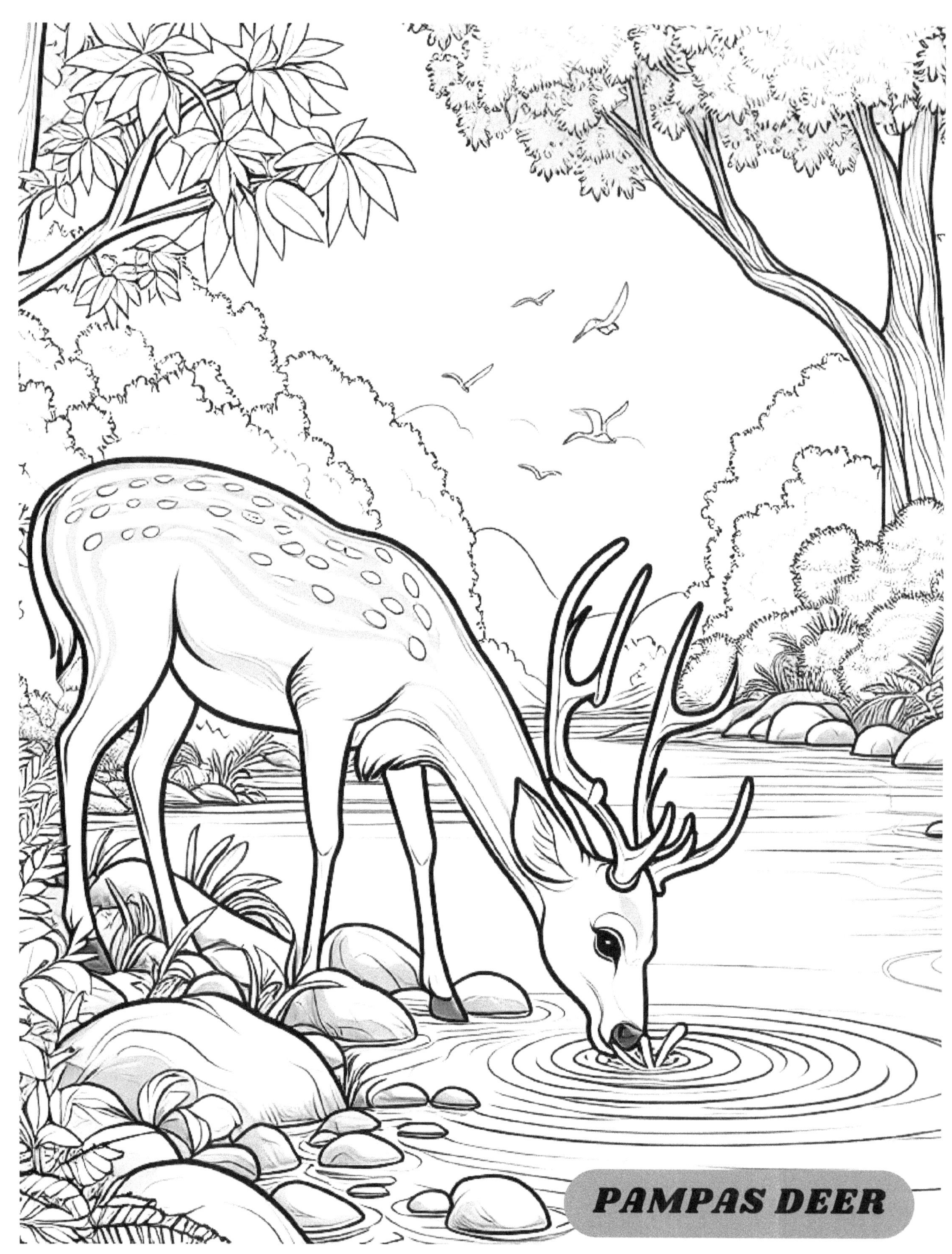
PAMPAS DEER

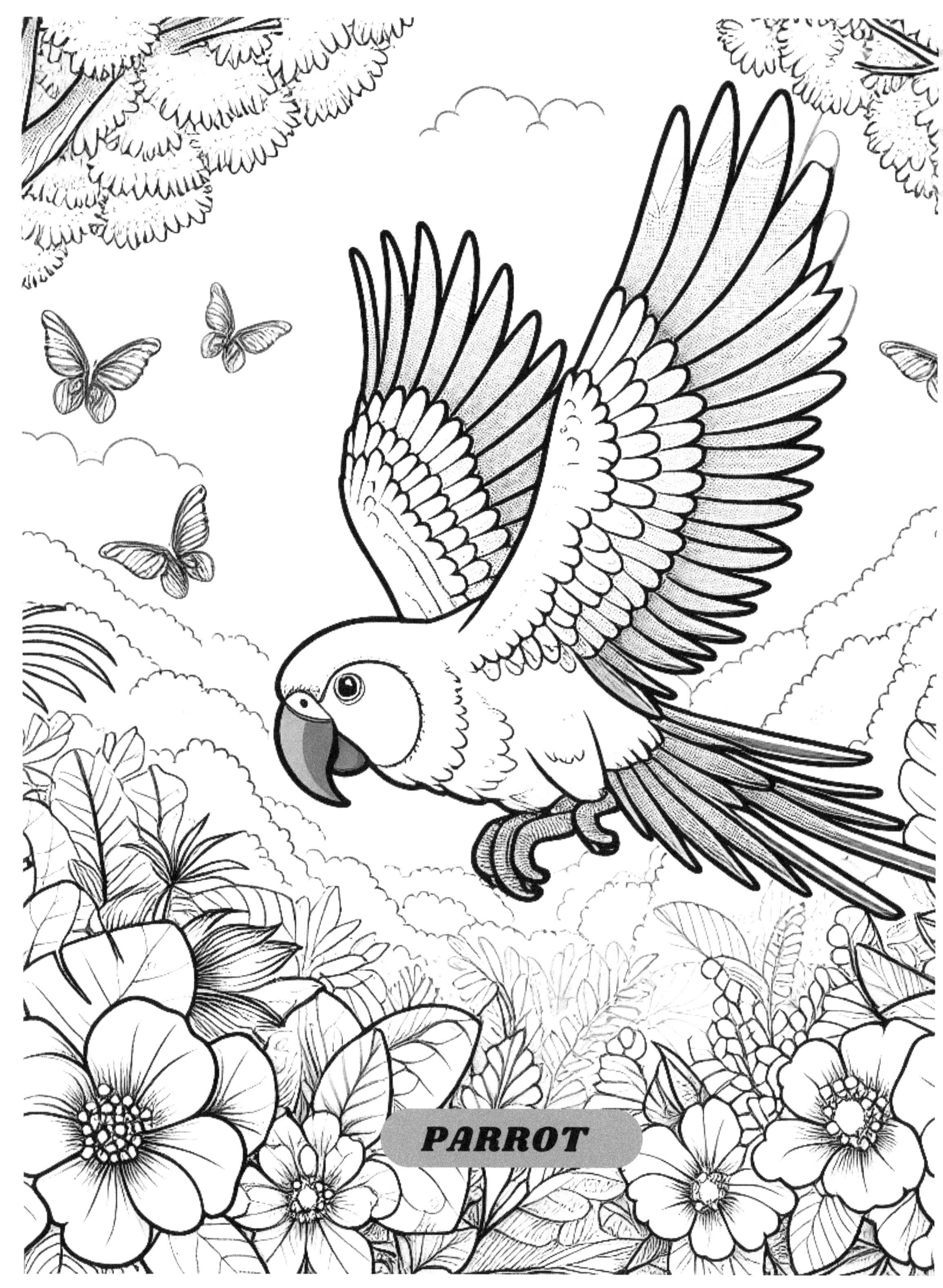
PARROT

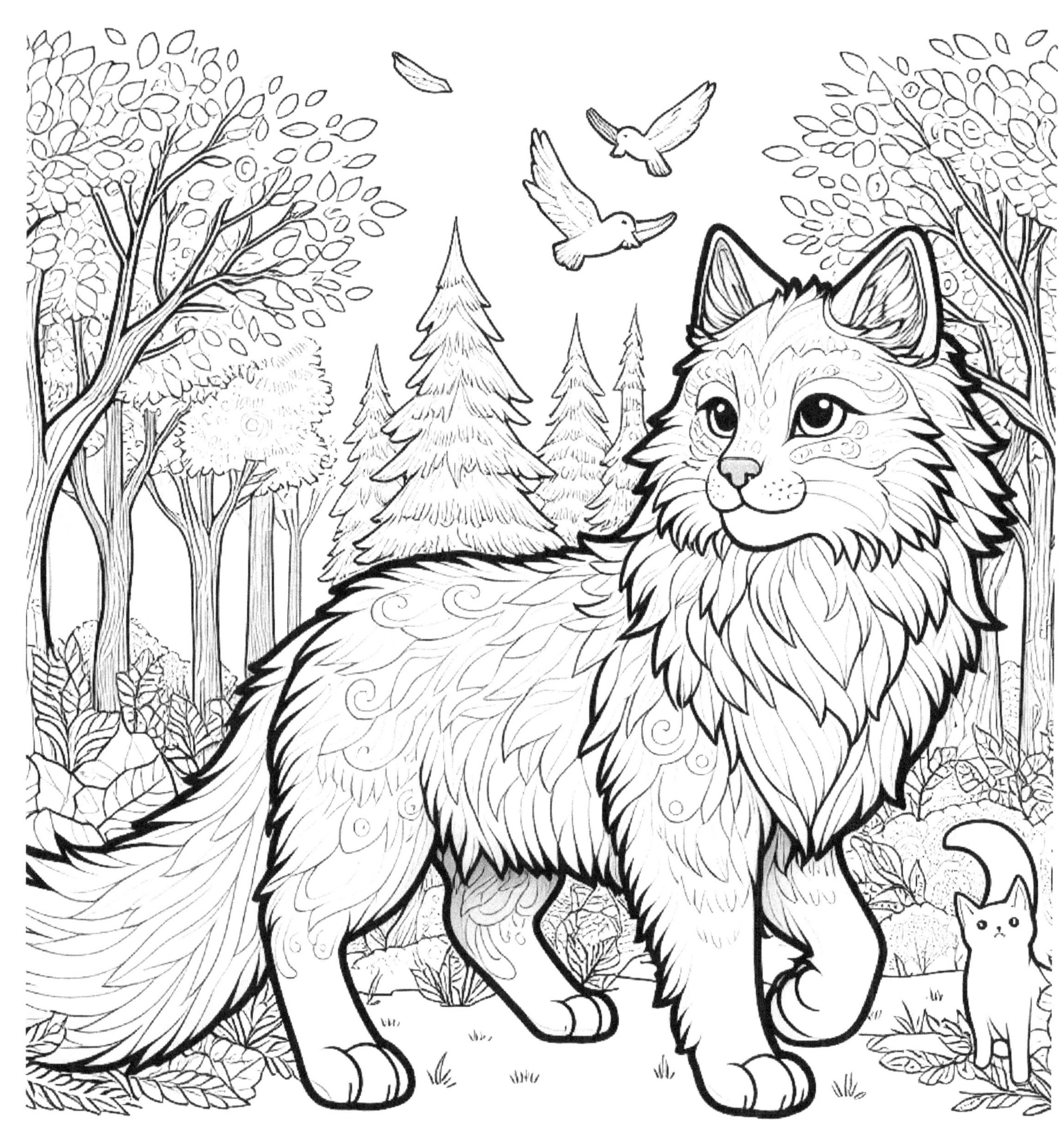

MARGAY CAT

CAXINGUELÊ
BRAZILIAN SQUIRREL

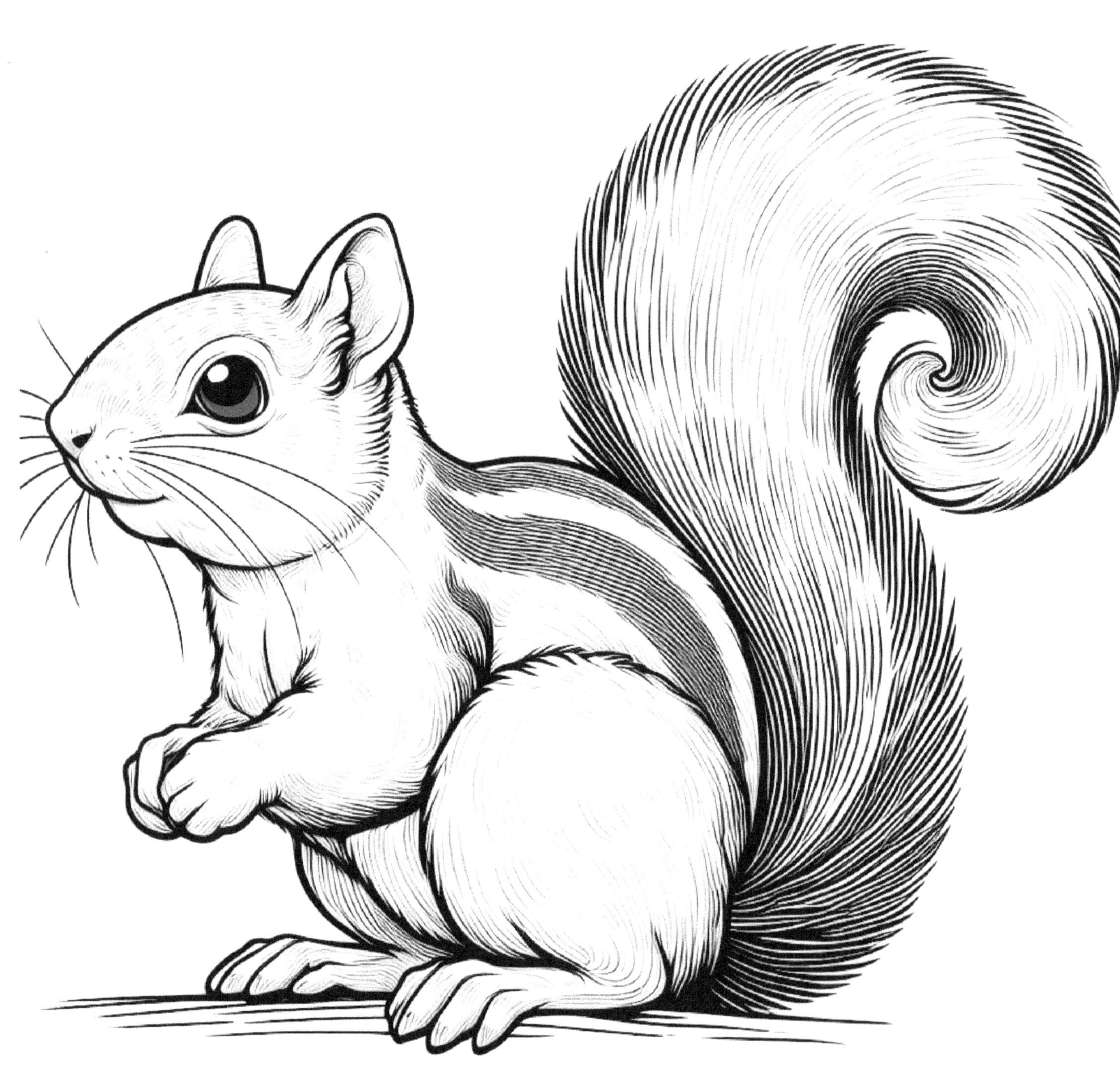

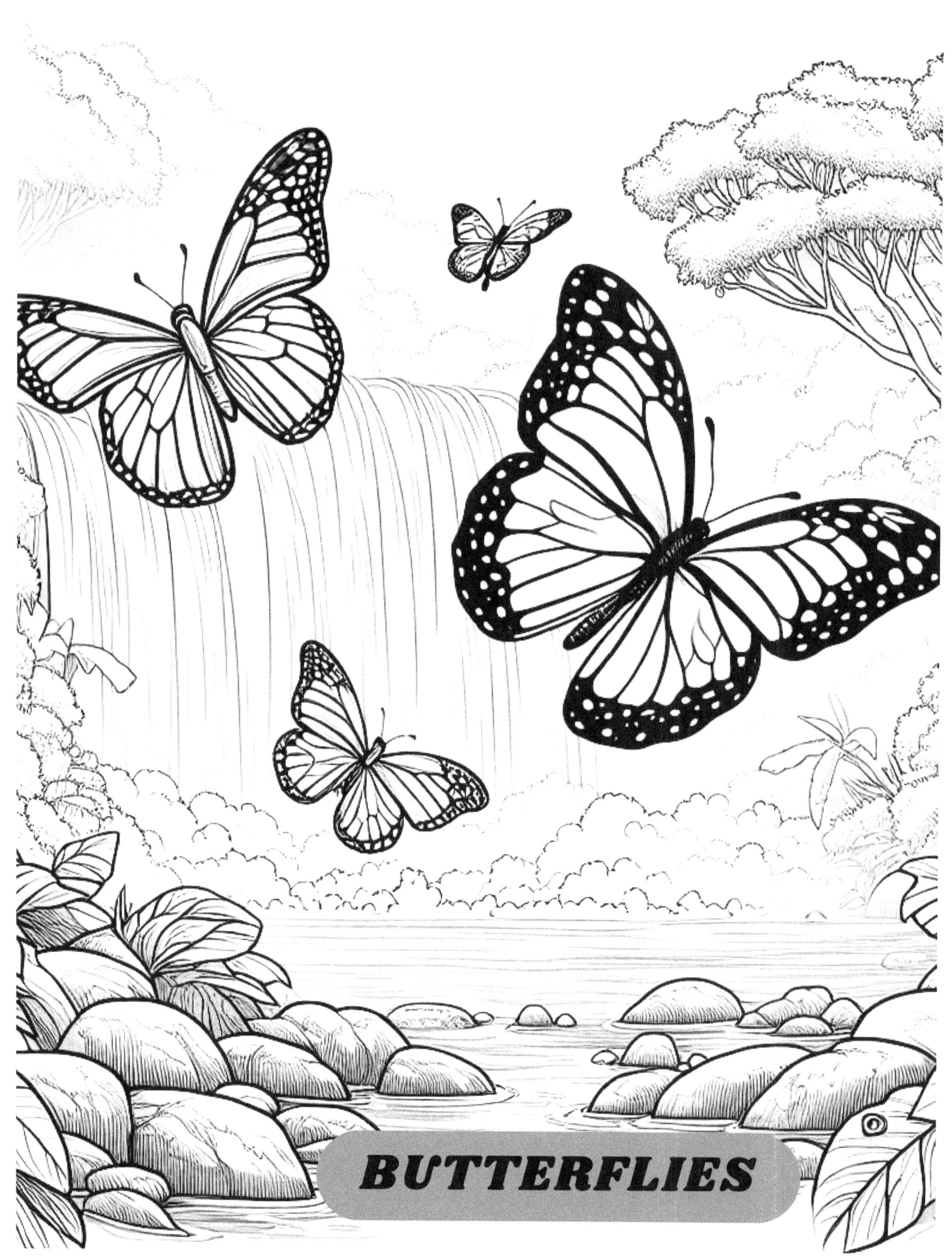
BUTTERFLIES

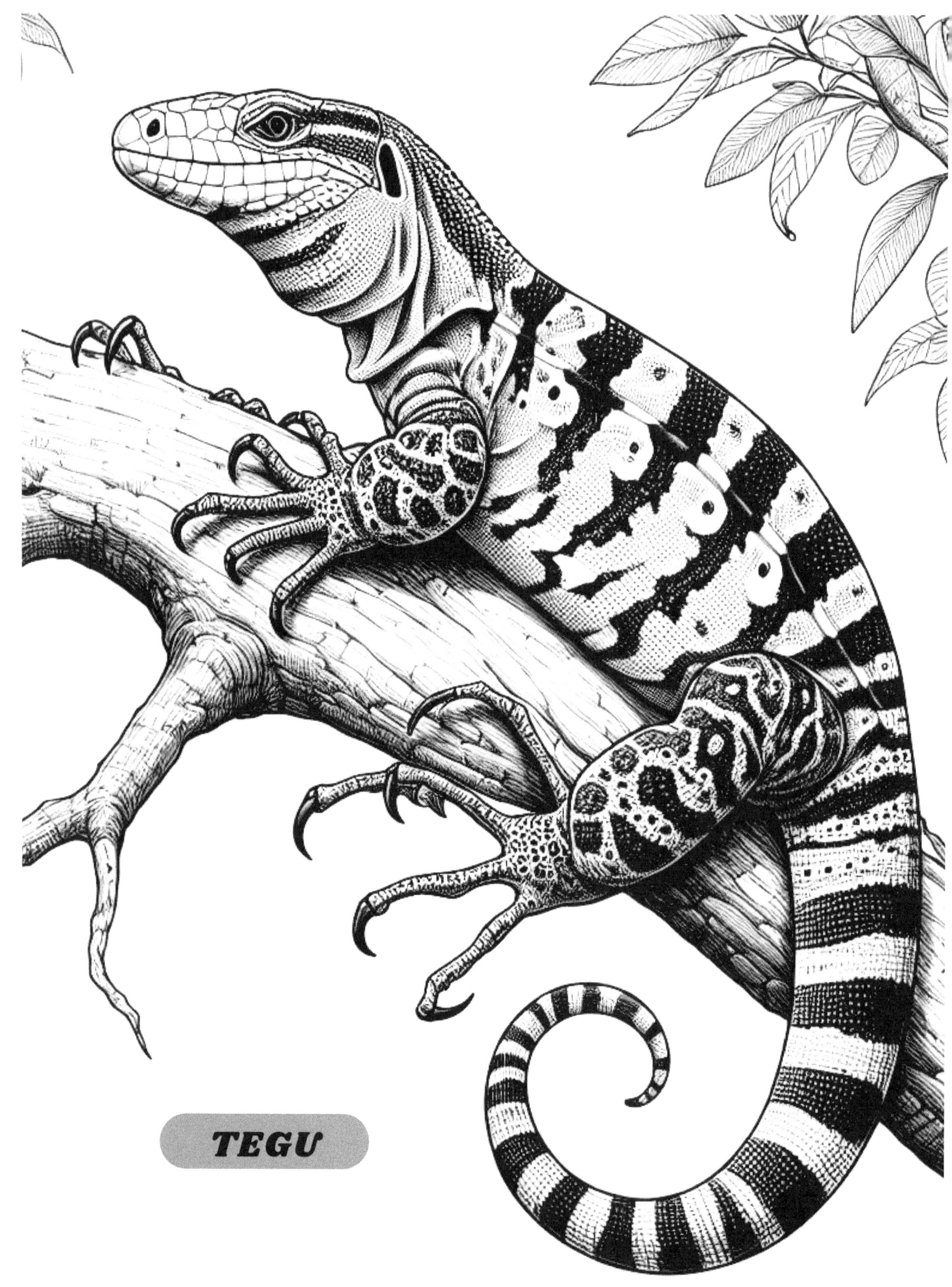
TEGU

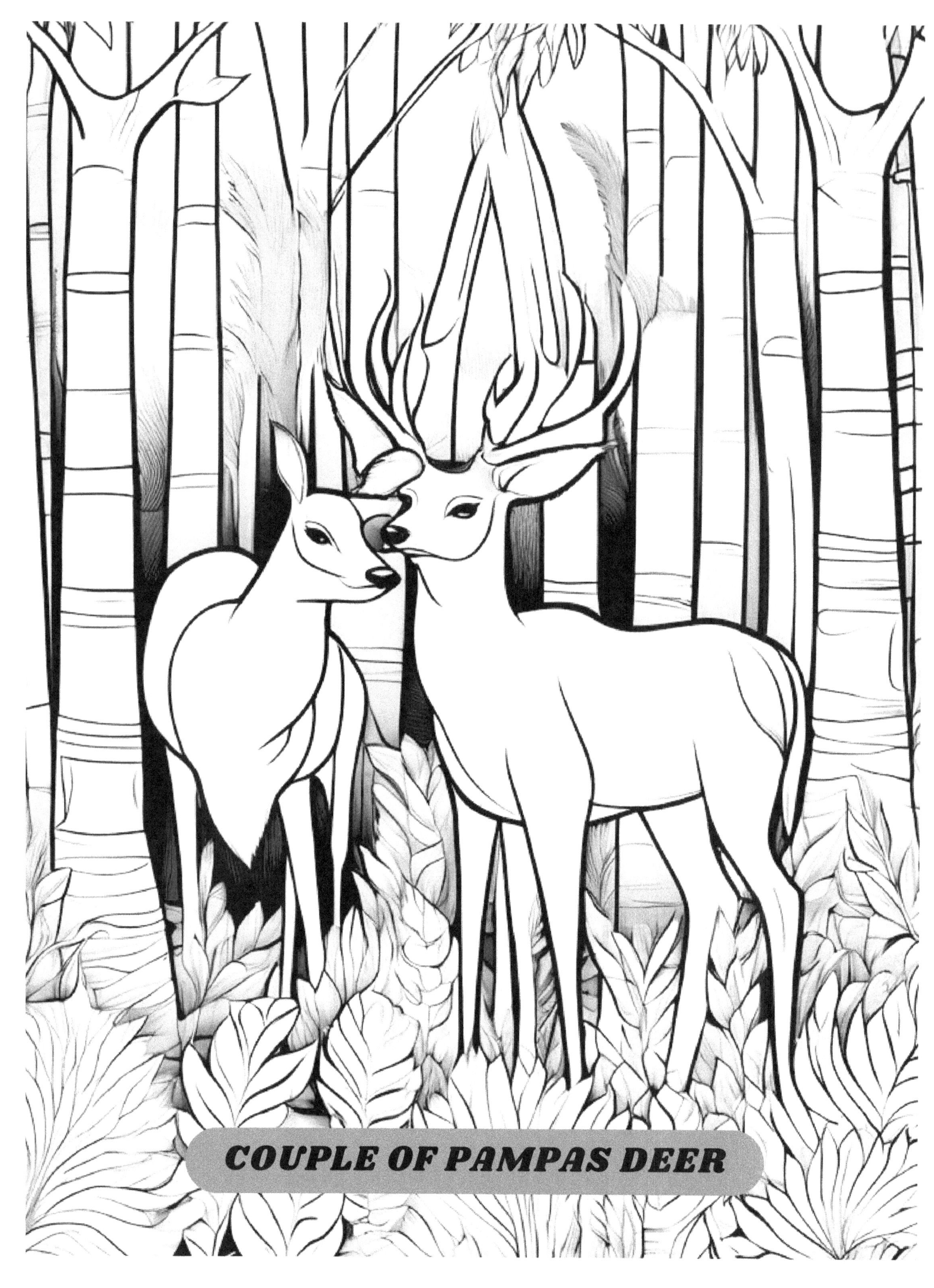

COUPLE OF PAMPAS DEER

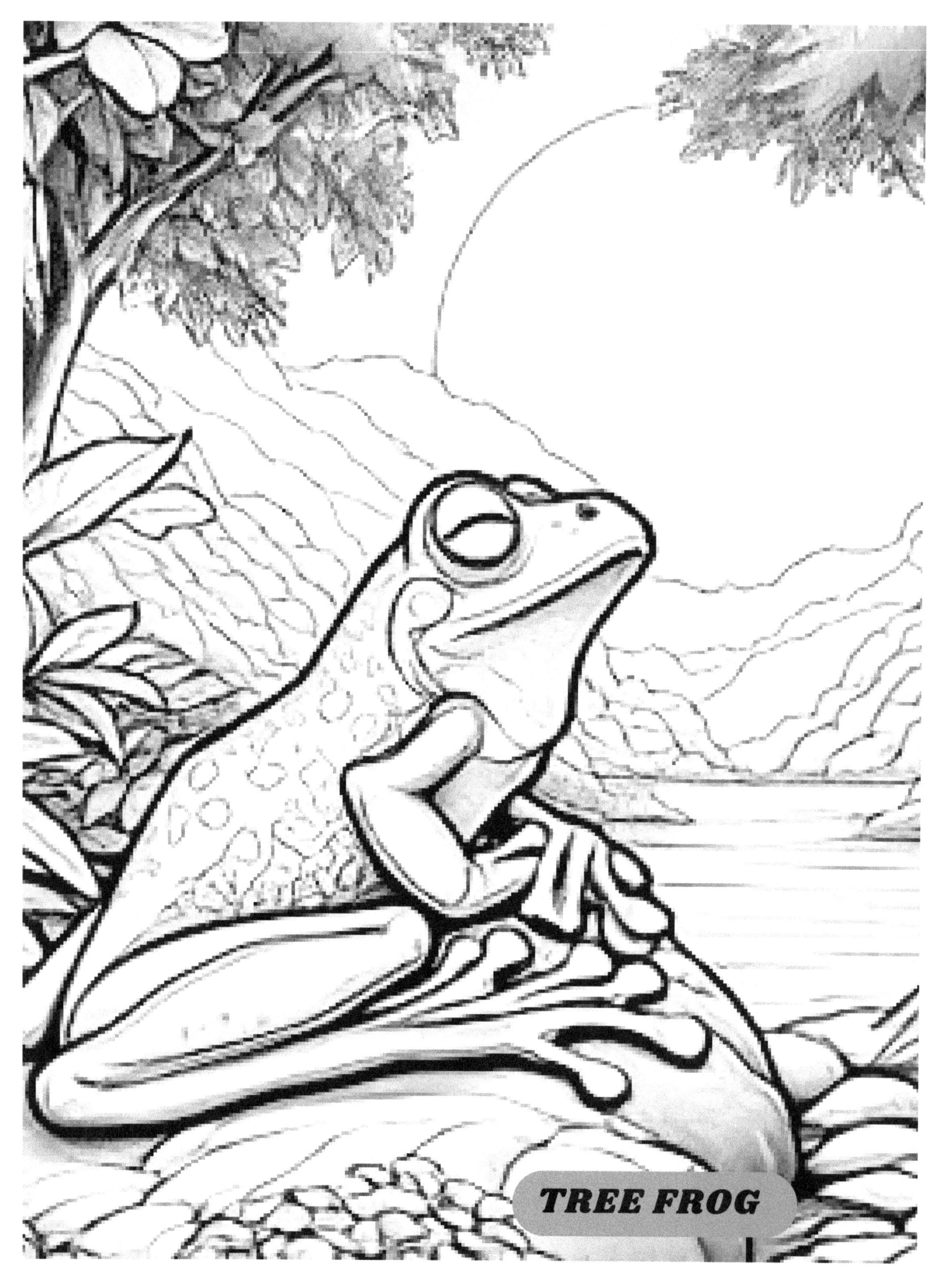
TREE FROG

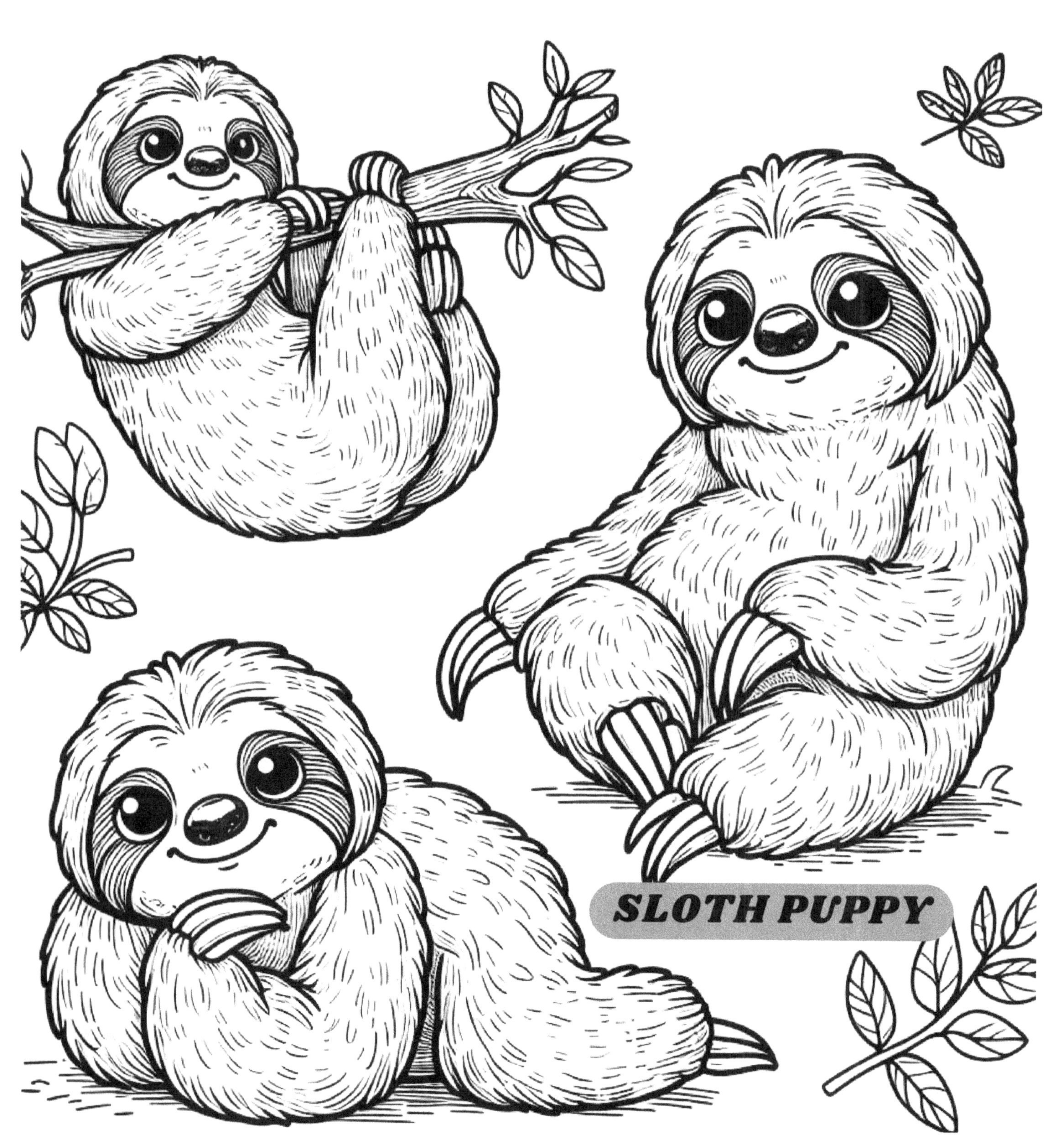
SLOTH PUPPY

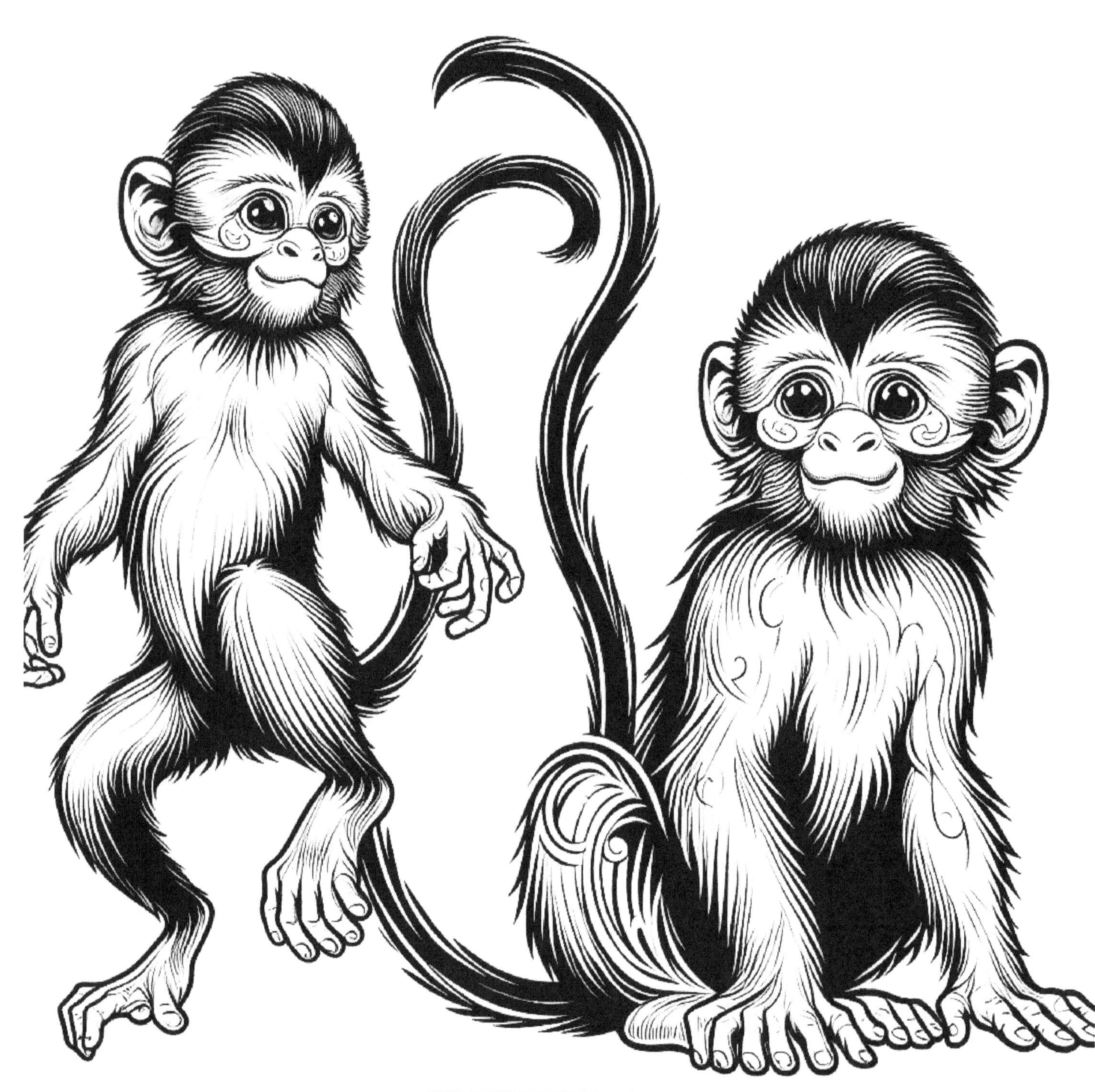

GUARIBA MACAQUE

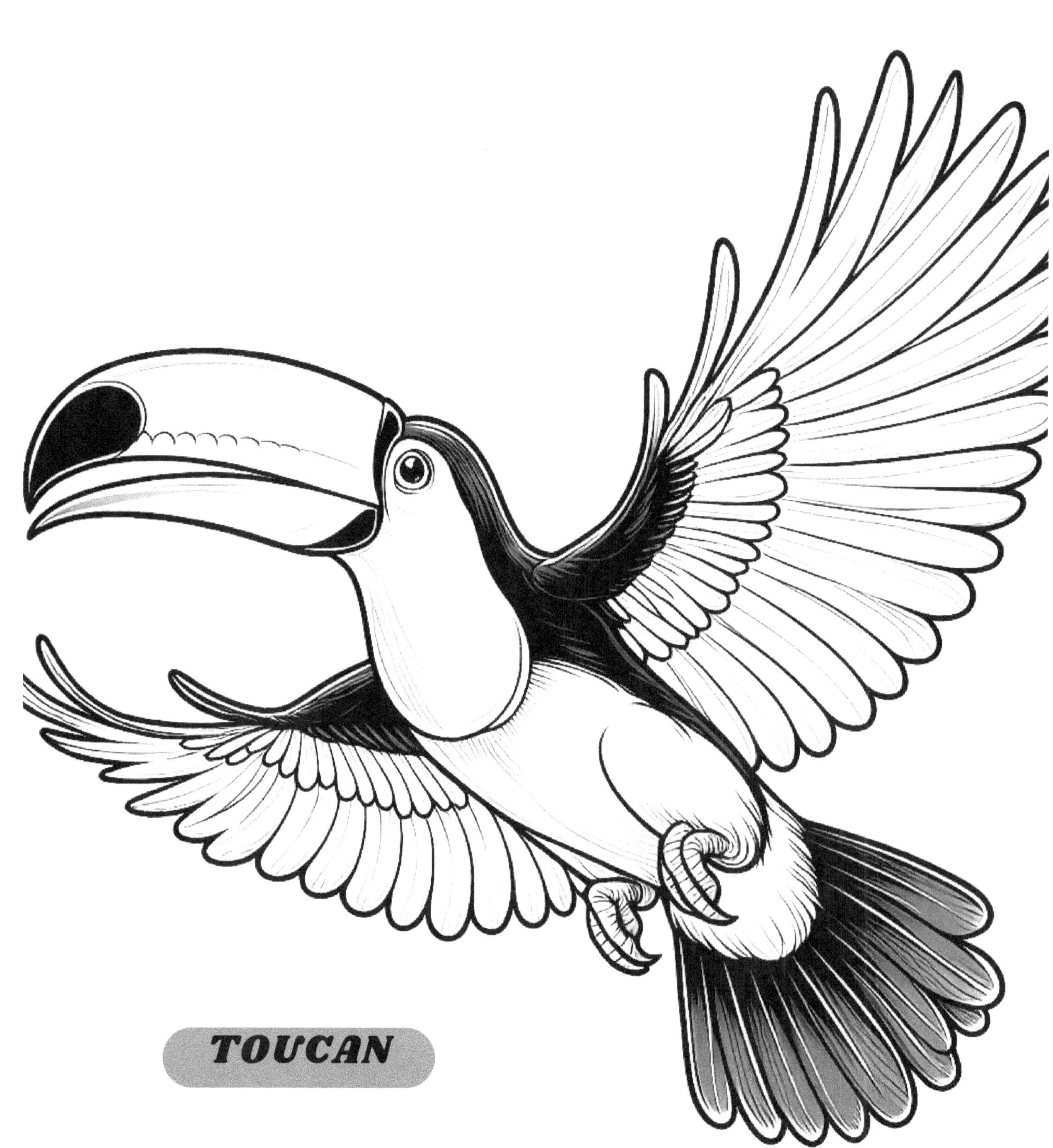

TOUCAN

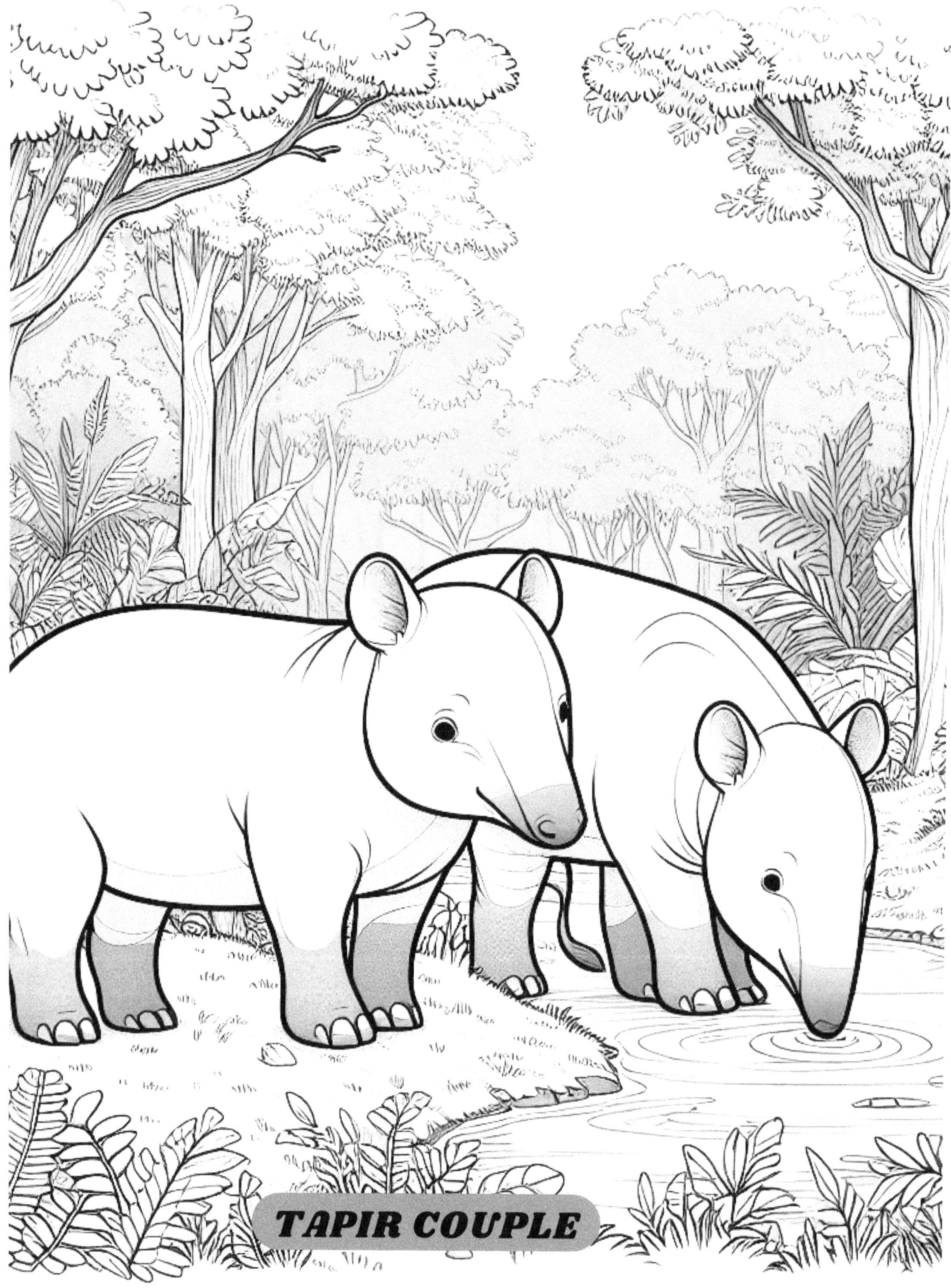

TAPIR COUPLE

JAGUAR FAMILY
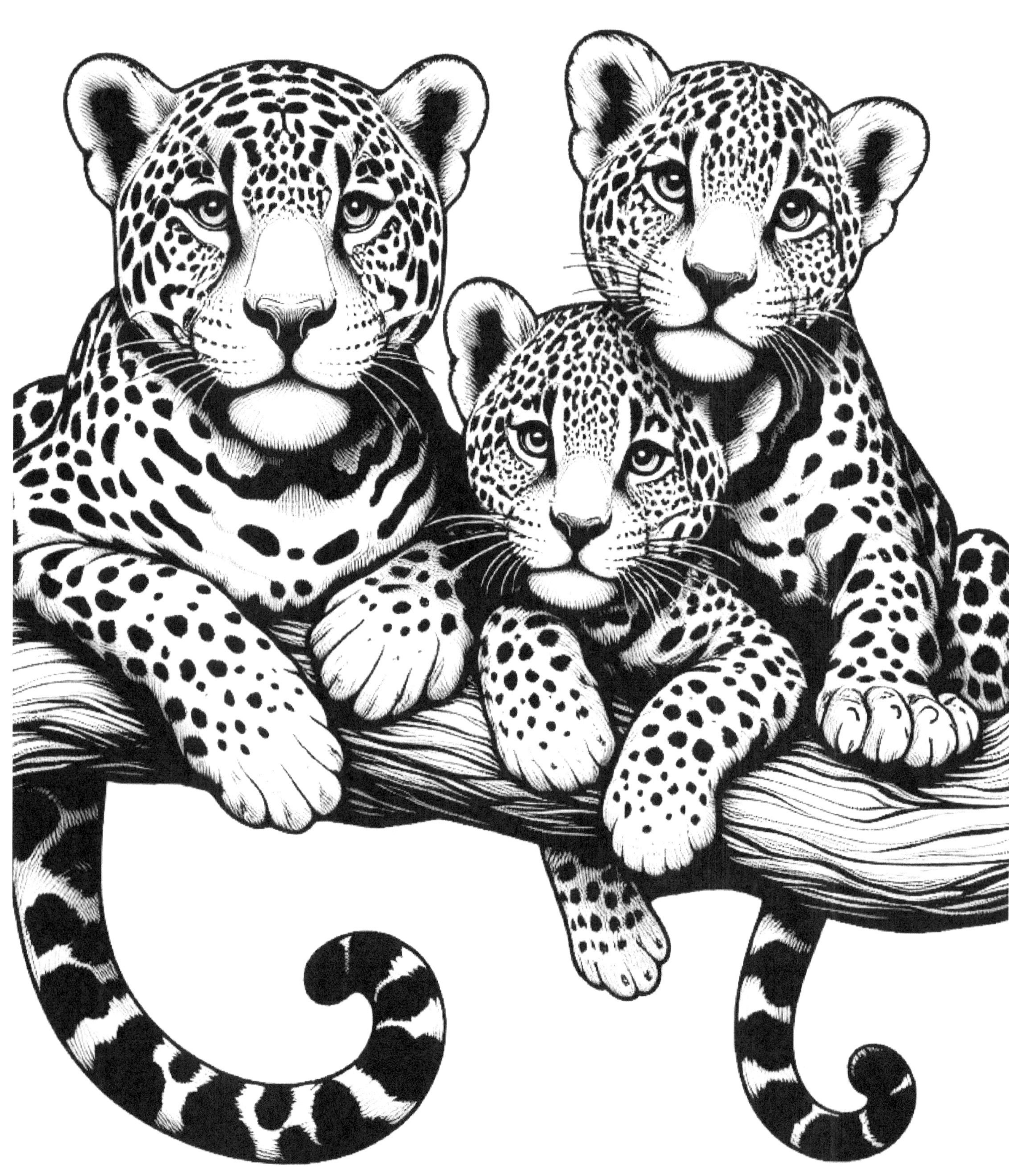

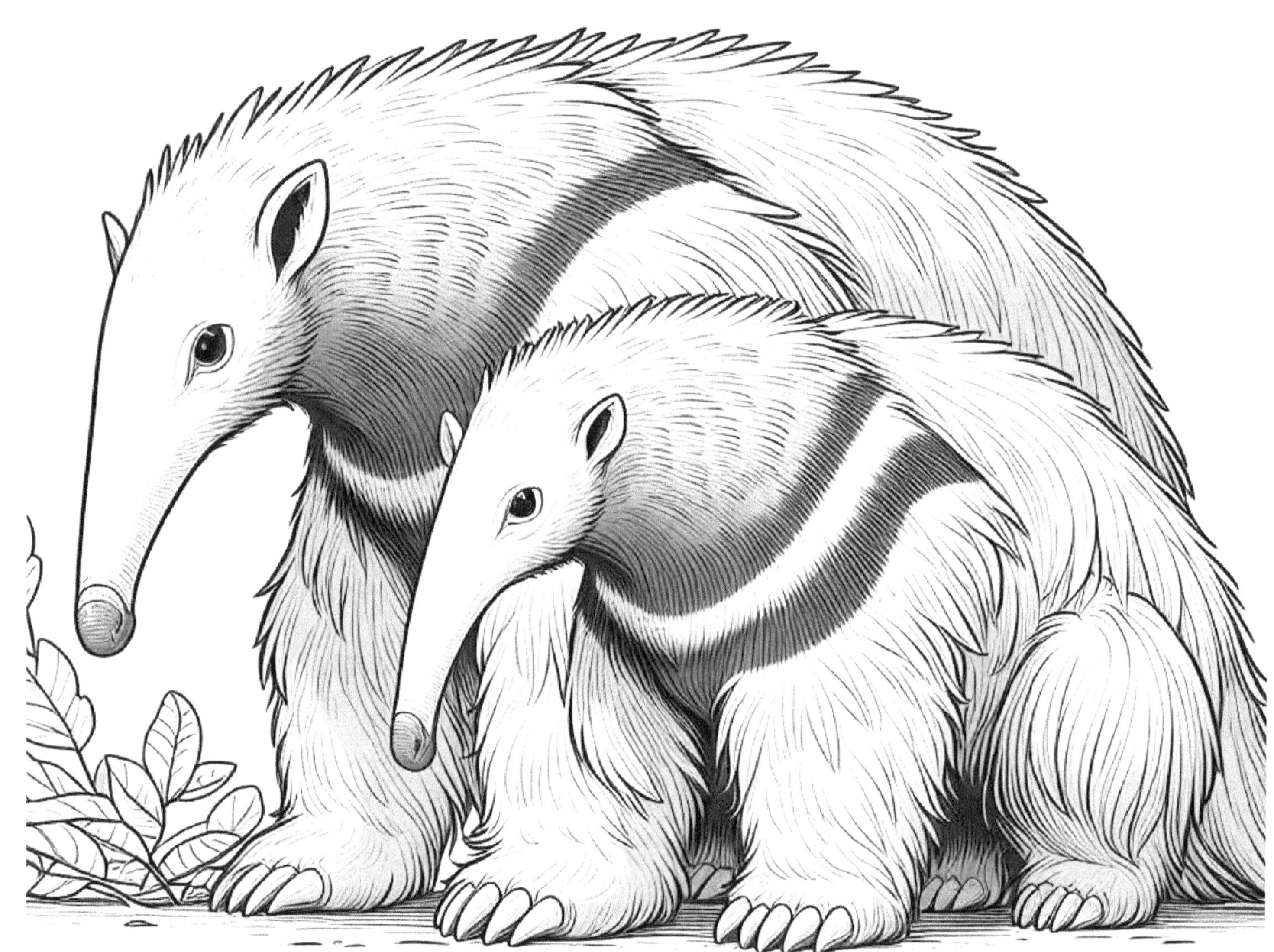

ANTEATER FLAG COUPLE

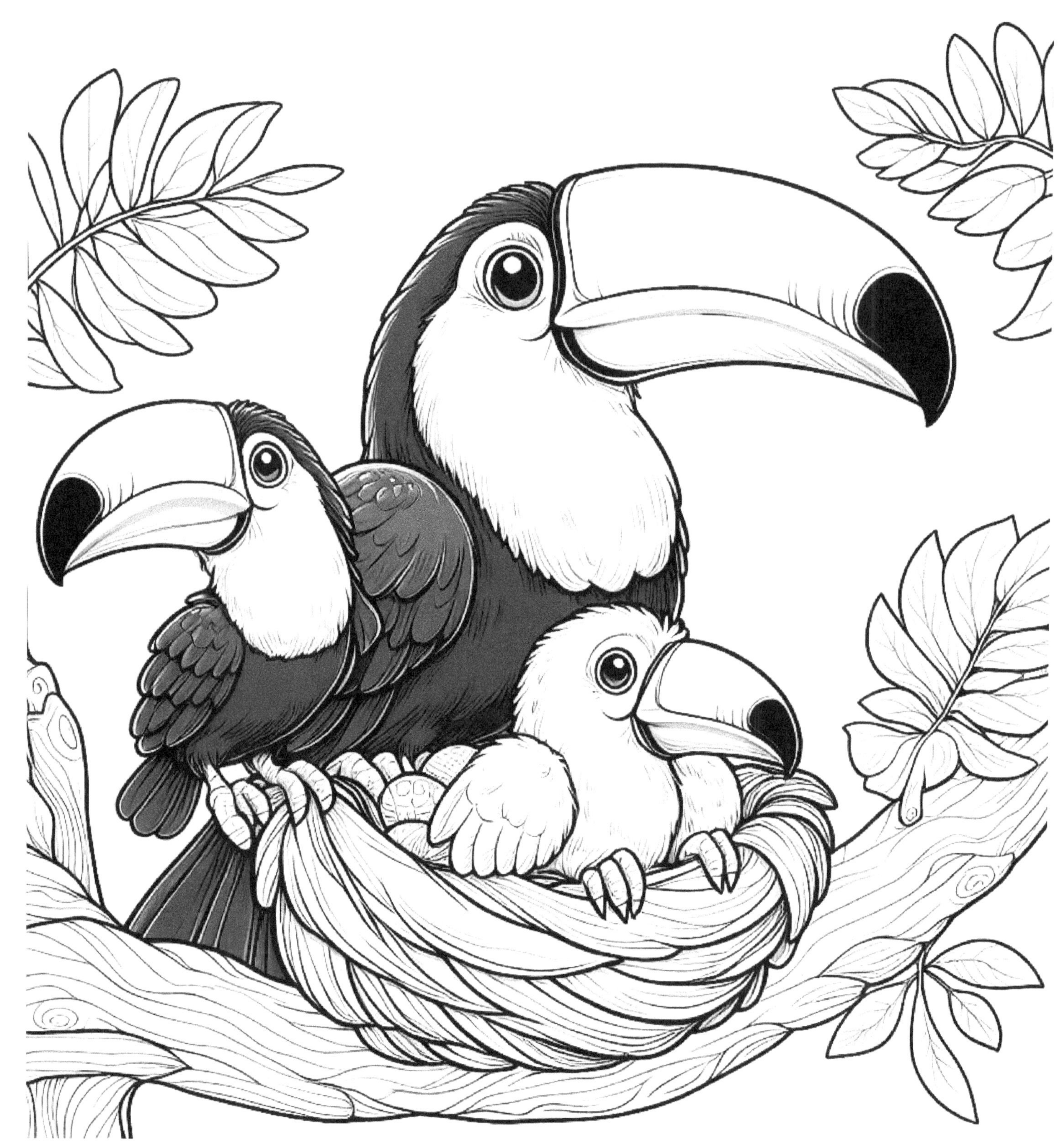

TOUCAN FAMILY

LANCEHEAD

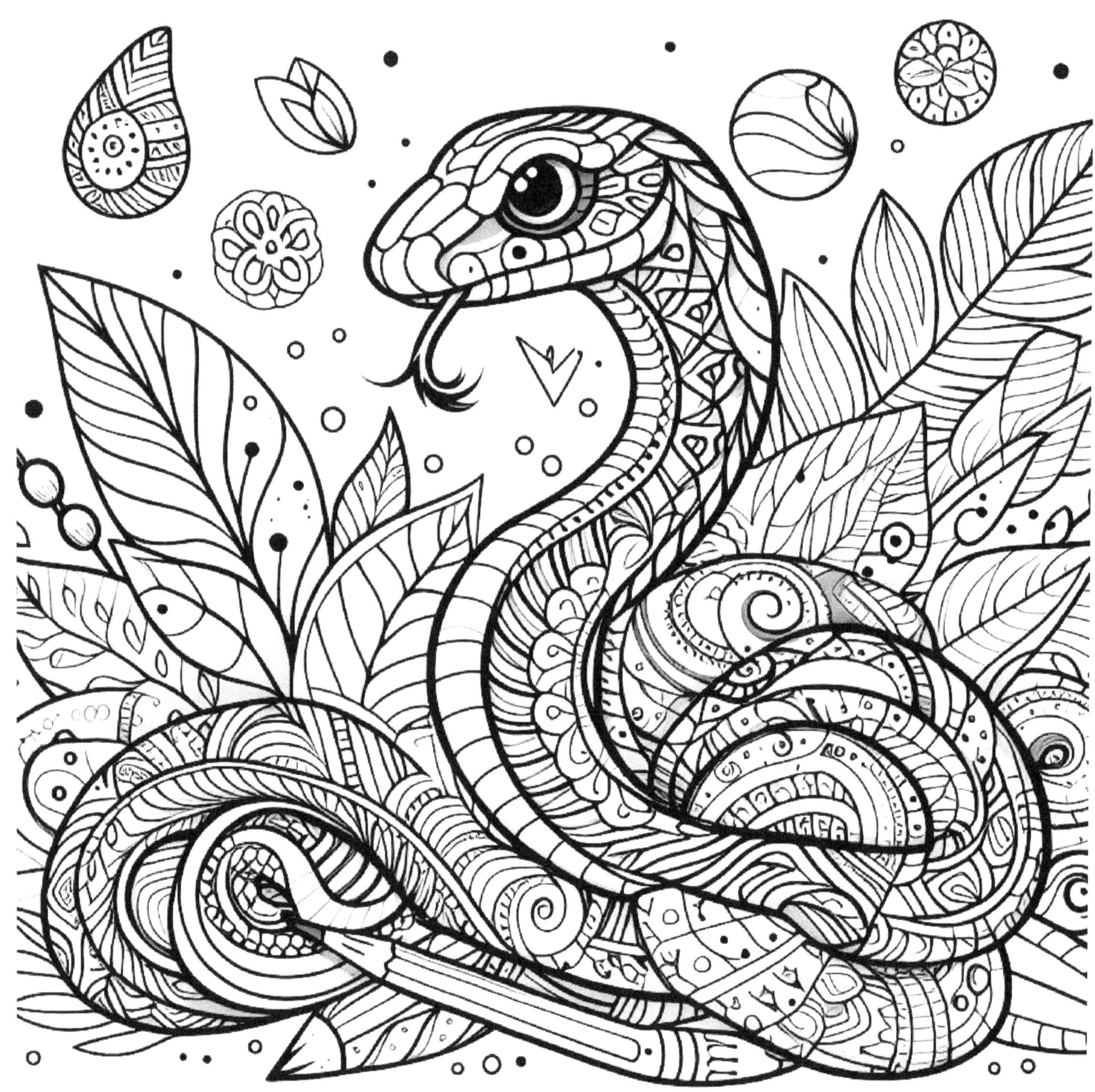